W9-BOO-380

KNACK
MAKE IT EASY

MEXICAN
COOKING

KNACK

MEXICAN
COOKING

A Step-by-Step Guide to Authentic Dishes Made Easy

Chelsie Kenyon

Photographs by Jackie Alpers

KNACK
MAKE IT EASY

Guilford, Connecticut
An imprint of Globe Pequot Press

To buy books in quantity for corporate use
or incentives, call **(800) 962-0973**
or e-mail **premiums@GlobePequot.com.**

Copyright © 2010 by Morris Book Publishing, LLC

ALL RIGHTS RESERVED. No part of this book may be reproduced or transmitted in any form by any means, electronic or mechanical, including photocopying and recording, or by any information storage and retrieval system, except as may be expressly permitted in writing from the publisher. Requests for permission should be addressed to Globe Pequot Press, Attn: Rights and Permissions Department, P.O. Box 480, Guilford, CT 06437.

Knack is a registered trademark of Morris Publishing Group, LLC, and is used with express permission.

Editor-in-Chief: Maureen Graney
Editor: Katie Benoit
Cover Design: Paul Beatrice, Bret Kerr
Interior Design: Paul Beatrice
Layout: Casey Shain
Cover photos by Jackie Alpers
Interior photos by Jackie Alpers

Library of Congress Cataloging-in-Publication Data is available on file.

ISBN 978-1-59921-780-2

The following manufacturers/names appearing in Knack Mexican Cooking are trademarks:
Cointreau®, Grand Marnier®, Popsicle®

Printed in China

10 9 8 7 6 5 4 3 2 1

The information in this book is true and complete to the best of our knowledge. All recommendations are made without guarantee on the part of the author or Globe Pequot Press. The author and Globe Pequot Press disclaim any liability in connection with the use of this information.

Acknowledgments

I first and foremost have to thank my husband Matthew for being patient and helpful while I tested these recipes and spent countless hours writing through the night. I have to give muchos gracias to my partner-in-crime, Jackie Alpers, who brought these recipes to life with her stunning photography. Thanks to everyone at Globe Pequot Press, especially Katie who patiently answered my endless questions and to Keith Wallman for introducing me into the world of writing cookbooks. Thanks to the "unspoken heroes" who worked on the layout and get a big thumbs up for bringing everything together.

Thanks to Barb Doyen for her support, assurance, and guidance. And this book would not be possible without the help of my mother, who helped me review each recipe to make sure it was exactly as it should be.

—Chelsie Kenyon

Photographer's Acknowledgments

I'd like to express my profound gratitude to my wonderful and amazingly talented editors at Globe Pequot Press, Katie Benoit and Keith Wallman; my equally wonderful and talented husband Jason Willis for all of his love and support; my mother Lois Ungar and brother Jonathan Alpers for teaching me how to cook and for developing my love of food; and Chelsie Kenyon for her insight and for being such an upbeat and positive person to work with. I also want to express my appreciation to H.F Coors China Manufacturers in Tucson for contributing most of the dishware featured in this book.

—Jackie Alpers

CONTENTS

INTRODUCTION

Traditional and authentic Mexican food is nothing like the commercial Mexican food found outside of the country. In Mexico you would be hard-pressed to find a processed corn-meal shell stuffed with overly seasoned ground beef and topped with shredded cheddar cheese. Things like nacho cheese and taco seasoning packets are virtually unknown in Mexico. What you will find are delicious regional dishes made with fresh, local ingredients that reflect the culture and history of the area.

Native Mexican Cuisine

Mexican cooking has a diverse history that began thousands of years ago with native Mexican ingredients such as beans, squash, and chiles. Corn began as a wild grass, and the indigenous people of Mexico domesticated it to create maize, which became an integral part of the native Mexican diet. The Aztec diet was anchored with maize that was treated and ground into dough to form corn cakes or tamales, and it was pressed out into thin tortillas. Chiles were added to just about every dish to add flavor and enliven the senses.

Spanish Influence

When the Spanish conquistadors arrived from Spain to take over Mexico, they found a culture rich with history and tradition. They were amazed at the variety of foods that the Aztecs enjoyed. Although they came into brief contact with the Mayans on the first expedition, it was with the Aztecs that the Spanish got a true taste of native Mexican cuisine. Even though the dishes were new and exciting, they longed for the foods of their homeland. The Spaniards began to import their Old World ingredients to Mexico and incorporated them into Mexican cuisine. One of the biggest contributions was the introduction of pigs and lard. Pork and the fat that is rendered from it dramatically changed Mexican cuisine.

Regional Cuisine

Because Mexico is so geographically diverse, each region has developed its own signature dishes that make use of each area's locally found resources and ingredients. Thanks to modern transportation local ingredients can now be shipped all over Mexico, so each region's style of cuisine is beginning to be available in other places. But to get the best

representation of regional fare, you have to go to the source and eat in the region where the particular dish you want to try is made.

Northern Mexico

Northern Mexico is known as the *frontera,* or frontier country, because of its close proximity to the U.S.–Mexico border. It has an arid desert climate, and the indigenous people of the area were hunter-gatherers. They hunted small game and wild turkey and ate cacti, insects, and wild fruit. Machaca was made by drying game meat such as deer and rabbit as a way to preserve it. After the Spanish arrived, they moved into the area and began raising cattle. These early Spanish cowboys learned the process of making machaca and used it to preserve the beef from their own cattle. Wheat was the grain of choice for the Spanish, and because they dominated the area, wheat quickly replaced corn, and flour tortillas became the bread of choice. The cowboys and ranchers grilled their meals outdoors over open fires and steamed them in pits dug into the ground. These rustic influences remain today, and the cuisine of Northern Mexico is based on this ranch-style cooking. Enchiladas, carne asada, and more recently burritos are all examples of dishes of Northern Mexico.

Central Mexico

Central Mexico has one of the most diverse regional cuisines in the country. Before the Spanish arrived, the area was home to the Aztecs. They created irrigation systems, so the area was abundant with fresh produce such as corn, tomatoes, tomatillos, avocados, chiles, coconuts, and pineapples. Beans were used as a protein source, as were insects and cacti. The Aztecs had a primarily vegetarian and low-fat diet, with small amounts of wild turkey, iguana, fish, and insects. When the Spanish arrived, they began to import pork, chicken, rice, onions, cinnamon, sugar, and more.

These ingredients were gradually incorporated into existing dishes and also led to the creation of new ones.

Central Mexico's fairly mild climate makes it an ideal location to grow a wide variety of fruits and vegetables. And its location has left it open to influences from the regional cuisines of the North and the South. The Spanish initially landed in Veracruz on the eastern coast, and it eventually became an international port. This, in turn, has led to Mediterranean influences on the cuisine of Veracruz, such as green olives and capers.

Southern Mexico and the Yucatan Peninsula

Southern Mexico has a wet, tropical climate that remains humid and warm all year round. While beef, pinto beans, and flour tortillas are favored in the northern regions, the southern areas favor chicken, black beans, and corn tortillas. The southern state of Oaxaca is known for its mole recipes. These complicated dishes featuring over thirty ingredients are the cornerstone of Oaxacan cuisine. In the Yucatan region the cuisine has not changed much from its ancient roots and still boasts many regional dishes that are not far from the dishes the Mayans enjoyed.

The Simplicity of Mexican Cuisine

Mexican food for the most part involves simple, flavorful ingredients prepared with traditional methods that are combined to create an authentic flavor for each dish. Though there are traditional Mexican dishes that are labor-intensive with multiple ingredients, most dishes are easy to prepare with local components. Even exotic-sounding ingredients such as banana leaves can be found with just a little effort or can be substituted with more common items such as parchment paper.

Mexican Food Is a Feast for the Senses

Mexican cuisine boasts a wide variety of dishes from hearty beef and chile dishes of the North to the exotic dishes of the South, which feature unique ingredients such as insects and squash blossoms. Whether you're looking for classic comfort food or searching for a daring culinary experience, you can find it all within the cuisine of Mexico.

COMAL

This traditional cast-iron griddle is used for grilling, heating, and searing

A comal is a heavy, cast-iron griddle that is a must-have for cooking authentic Mexican food. It is used for cooking many items on the stovetop and can also be used in the oven. Comals come in all shapes and sizes, but the two most common are an oval shape that can be used over two burners on a regular stove and a smaller round shape used over one burner.

Before you use your comal for the first time, you must "season" it. This will clean it and prepare the cast iron for use. In order to season your comal, you will need to rinse it with plenty of warm water. Dry it thoroughly and then rub it down with cooking oil or lard. Bake it in a 350°F oven for 1 hour. Remove it from the oven, let it cool, and then rub it

Large Comal

- A large comal is perfect for larger items such as large pieces of beef or pork.

- Large comals are also great for cooking large amounts of food for an entire meal.

- A large comal is very heavy, so take care not to drop it. The comal may cause damage to the floor or whatever it is dropped on.

Small Comal

- Smaller comals are easier to handle because they weigh less.

- Small, round comals are a perfect size to cook or re-heat a tortilla. In most Mexican kitchens, comals

  are used for that purpose on a daily basis.

- The handle will also heat up while using it, so please use a towel or oven mitt if you need to move it during the cooking process.

down with a cloth to remove any residue. Repeat this process again, and your comal is ready for use.

Comals impart wonderful flavors to the food cooked on them. The more it is used, the better the flavors become. To clean a comal, simply wipe it down—do not use soap.

ZOOM

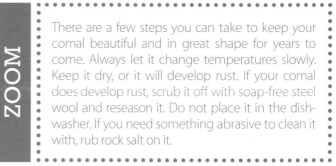

There are a few steps you can take to keep your comal beautiful and in great shape for years to come. Always let it change temperatures slowly. Keep it dry, or it will develop rust. If your comal does develop rust, scrub it off with soap-free steel wool and reseason it. Do not place it in the dishwasher. If you need something abrasive to clean it with, rub rock salt on it.

Oiling the Comal

- Rubbing a thin coat of oil over the surface will help repel water and prevent rust.

- The oil will also help create a nonstick surface.

- The more times the comal is heated with oil on it, the more the oil will soak into the cast iron and seal it so that over time you won't have to reseason it as often.

- Be sure to oil the entire pan— bottom, top, and handle.

Comal on Stove Top

- Comals can be used to cook just about anything you would cook in a regular pan, such as chicken, steak, or eggs.

- Comals are excellent for searing items over high heat on the stove and then transferred to an oven to finish the cooking.

- Cast iron retains heat and evenly disperses it to the items being cooked, so a comal is an excellent choice for just about any stove-top cooking.

MOLCAJETE

This traditional stone Mexican mortar and pestle tool is used for grinding authentic ingredients

Molcajetes have been used for thousands of years throughout Mexico to grind a wide variety of items such as dried corn, herbs, and chiles. The bowl portion of this tool is referred to as the molcajete and the handheld grinding stone is the tejolote. Modern appliances, such as a food processor or a blender, are quicker and more efficient, but grinding ingredients by hand in a molcajete coaxes out more complex and intricate flavors.

Authentic molcajetes are made from high-quality volcanic rock called basalt. Basalt's rough texture makes it ideal for grinding and blending a wide variety of ingredients. Sometimes the basalt may also have quartz or granite in it. Smooth

KNACK MEXICAN COOKING

Molcajete

- Use any type of rice to grind in the molcajete to clean it before the first use.

- To grind the rice, push down on the telojote while twisting it into the rice.

- Use the telojote to move the rice around between grinding so that you are grinding it evenly.

- Grind the rice all over the interior surface of the molcajete. You may need to tip it to the side to grind the rice onto the surfaces near the edges.

Decorative Molcajete

- Decorative molcajetes are pieces of art. They are hand carved, and each one is unique.

- Even though they are wonderful pieces of art, they should be used and cared for like any other molcajete.

- There are a large variety of designs available from artisans, but take care to choose one that is the correct size for your needs, rather than your favorite design.

basalt molcajetes are also available and are a great choice for most grinding purposes.

To get your molcajete ready for use, grind $1/2$ cup rice for 10 to 15 minutes and discard. Repeat this process until the rice does not pick up any gray discoloration or grit from the stone. Beware of products made with inferior rock, as the rock will grind off into the ingredient, creating grit in the finished item.

Before purchasing a molcajete, make sure the product is authentic, hand carved, and made in Mexico.

ZOOM

Molcajetes come in many shapes, sizes, and textures. Small molcajetes are ideal for grinding small amounts of herbs. Larger, deeper styles are perfect for grinding larger amounts of grains or ingredients. Most molcajetes are basic, consisting of a plain bowl shape with three short legs and a bell- or bat-shaped tejolote. Unique decorative varieties may include a hand-carved head of a pig or bull.

Smooth Molcajete

- If you are going to be using your molcajete on a regular basis, choose one that you feel comfortable leaving on the countertop, as they can be heavy and difficult to move around.

- Some molcajetes of the smoother variety are often painted on the exterior. They look great sitting out in the kitchen and stand ready for use any time you need it.

Molcajete Used to Make Salsa

- When shopping for a molcajete, consider what you will be using it for to help you decide which size to get.

- If you are going to be using it primarily for grinding spices, a small version is suitable and easy to move around and store.

- If you are going to be using it for grinding things such as salsas and guacamoles, a medium or large molcajete is appropriate, although some of the larger ones can be heavy to move around.

OLLA

This traditional and beautiful Mexican clay pot is used to cook beans and more

An olla is a very large and deep clay pot with two small handles and a fitted lid. It is often a very decorative piece with hand-painted flowers and/or vines decorating the outside of the pot and the lid.

Ollas are handmade items fired at very low temperatures to create an earthenware pot. Earthenware is very porous and will absorb the subtle flavors of the items you cook in it. The more you use it, the more it will impart a unique flavor to your food. Traditionally an olla is used to cook beans, but it can also be used to make coffee and stews.

Because ollas are fired at a low temperature, they are very fragile and can chip easily. They are also sensitive to sudden

Olla

- Ollas are beautiful pieces of cookware that are hand painted and look great on display.

- The brightly colored flowers and woven vines that decorate most ollas are a

representation of traditional Mexican style.

- If you have a lot of uses for an olla, you may want to have an extra one on hand in case you need to use more than one at a time.

Inside of an Olla

- Ollas are traditionally large and deep and hold roughly the capacity of the average stockpot.

- Ollas can be made with or without handles. The handles get hot with the rest of the pot, so use a thick towel or a pot holder when moving a hot olla from one place to another.

temperature changes, so make sure to start with a cool oven and let your olla heat up as the oven does. Unglazed pots absorb liquid and will create a steaming effect during cooking, however a glazed pot is easier to clean.

The FDA recommends not using a pot that is labeled "for decoration only" to cook in, since the glaze most likely contains lead. Look for an olla that is labeled "lead free" or "sin plomo."

ZOOM

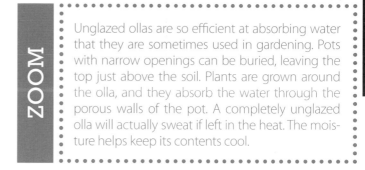

Unglazed ollas are so efficient at absorbing water that they are sometimes used in gardening. Pots with narrow openings can be buried, leaving the top just above the soil. Plants are grown around the olla, and they absorb the water through the porous walls of the pot. A completely unglazed olla will actually sweat if left in the heat. The moisture helps keep its contents cool.

Uses for an Olla

- One of the best uses for an olla is cooking delicious beans.

- You can simmer the beans over low heat on the stove top or you can slow cook them in the oven at very low heat, around 200 to 250°F.

- Although many recipes are called frijoles de la olla, which means "beans that are cooked in an olla," the recipe often suggests cooking in a metal pot. True frijoles de la olla are cooked in a traditional earthenware pot.

Cleaning an Olla

- Before you use your olla for the first time, soak it in room-temperature water for about 30 minutes and then dry it with a towel.

- If you are going to cook with an unglazed pot, soak it for 20 minutes before each use.

- An olla should never be put in the dishwasher. Just soak it in warm water and use a towel to help remove excess food or water.

- Using anything abrasive could damage the glaze or ruin the surface of an unglazed olla.

TORTILLADORA

Use this tortilla press to flatten masa into a round tortilla

A *tortilladora* is a must-have item for preparing authentic homemade tortillas. A small ball of masa is placed between two flat plates, and a lever is used to press the two plates together, flattening the dough into a perfect circle.

Modern tortilladoras are made from cast iron and painted silver to prevent rusting. These cast-iron models are very heavy to move around, but the weight makes the pressing

job easier. Another less-favored choice is a tortilladora made from aluminum. It is lightweight and easy to move, but it takes a bit more effort to press the tortilla, and if you press too hard, you could actually snap the lever.

There are also wooden tortilladoras available, but some of them are bulky and take up a lot of space. A hardwood, such as oak, is usually used to make these wooden presses. Plastic

A Cast-iron Tortilla Press

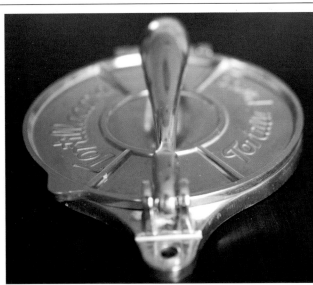

- Cast-iron presses are by far the most popular choice for everyday use.

- Since the cast iron is a heavy material, it will take very little pressure to press out the tortilla.

- The cast-iron press is fairly small, so it is easy to store, but the lever makes it difficult to stack anything on top of it. A small shelf is an easy solution. Store the press under the shelf, then you can easily stack other items on top.

A Basic Wooden Tortilla Press

- A wooden press can be made very simply with just a couple of pieces of wood plates and a longer piece for a handle.

- Some wooden presses are more detailed, with a base or feet and beveled edges.

- Some wooden presses are stained or glazed so they have a shiny surface.

- As with a metal press, just wipe down the surface after each use and allow it to dry before closing and storing it.

is the latest option, but it is not very sturdy.

In order to use a press, you will need to cover the two flat surfaces with plastic wrap or a large clear plastic bag. This helps you to remove the tortilla from the press and makes for easy cleanup. After you have prepared your tortilladora with the plastic, you can add the dough and press as usual. Tortilladoras are primarily used for corn tortillas.

ZOOM

Tortilladoras do not require much care. If you use plastic to cover the surface, there is virtually no cleanup. Just throw away the plastic and wipe down the lever. Cast-iron tortilladoras are heavy, so take care not to drop them, or they will likely crack or chip. If your tortilladora gets any food on it then simply wipe it down with a damp towel, do not submerge it in water.

Using a Tortilla Press

- For the average tortilla press, the ball of dough should be about the size of a walnut or slightly smaller.

- When the dough is pressed, it should be large enough to cover the pressing plate, but it should not quite make it to the edge.

- If dough presses out of the sides of the press, the dough ball was too large.

Caring for Your Tortilla Press

- The plastic is used to prevent the dough from sticking to the press and makes it easy to transition the tortilla to the comal to be cooked.

- Even though the dough is not really touching the press, it should still be wiped down after each use, especially the handle.

- If you take good care of your tortilladora, it will last a lifetime.

MOLINILLO

This decorative Mexican wooden whisk is used to add froth to hot beverages

Molinillos were first used in Mexico around two hundred years ago and were very simple in design. They were basically just a wooden handle with a small piece of carved wood at the end and used to add foam to hot chocolate. The molinillos you can find these days are almost works of art with the decorative carvings and burnt-on designs. The more recent versions also have loose, wooden rings around the bottom, which help add even more froth.

Before the invention of the molinillo, froth was added by pouring chocolate from cup to cup. Then it was discovered that sticks with twigs could be used to stir the drink and create the froth. That led to the creation of the molinillo.

Molinillo

- Molinillos are easily found in most Latin American markets as well as from many online resources.

- Molinillos range in price from $5 to $20, depending on the intricacy of the carvings and the attention to detail.

- There are two types of decoration for the molinillo: carved and burned. While the burned designs can bring out the beauty in the carved areas, they do nothing to help the froth. The carved areas create the foam.

Using the Molinillo

- With a molinillo your movements need to be quick, but steady. Keep a firm grip on the handle or you will splash chocolate all over the place.

- Quickly roll the handle between your palms while also moving the decorative end around the pot.

- The chocolate should be about 2 to 4 inches deep for maximum froth.

- Some molinillos have a flat bottom, almost like a foot, that can be used to steady it.

To use a molinillo, place the decorative end into a pot of Mexican hot chocolate. Place the handle between your palms and then quickly rub your hands together, causing the handle to spin back and forth. Continue to spin the molinillo until the hot chocolate is frothy.

Molinillos are a prized and cherished part of Mexican history, and there is even a popular children's song called "Bate, Bate Chocolate" ("Stir the Chocolate"). Children sing and move their hands as if they were using a molinillo.

ZOOM

Molinillos are made from wood carved with a technique called "turning." This creates many intricate surfaces that whip air into the chocolate better. The best way to clean a molinillo is to rinse it off with hot water and towel dry. Do not leave the molinillo sitting in liquid, as it could damage the wood. A molinillo will stain and become darker with use, which is perfectly normal.

Adding Froth

- Creating froth can take anywhere from 1 to 5 minutes, depending on the thickness of the chocolate, the depth of the liquid, and the quickness of movement.

- At first you will notice a small amount of white foam gathering around the edges of the pot.

- Gradually the foam will spread inward and cover the entire pot of chocolate.

Frothy and Delicious

- While using a molinillo in a pot of shallow liquid is the most effective way to use it, you can also use it for a single serving.

- If using it for a single serving, choose a large mug and only fill it half way. Froth the chocolate as desired and then slowly pour more chocolate into the side of the mug so as to not disperse the foam.

- Using a molinillo not only adds a distinctive flair to Mexican chocolate, it is also fun.

CAZUELA
Use this large, round cooking dish on the stove top and for baking

Cazuelas are another type of earthenware used in Mexican cooking. These clay dishes are wide and shallow and, like the olla, are low-fired to create an earthenware dish.

Cazuelas are often decorated on the inside of the dish as well as on the outside, and in some cases they are more of an artistic piece than something to cook with. When you buy a cazuela, make sure it is labeled "food safe" or "sin-plomo"

("lead free"), as many earthenware items made in Mexico use glaze that contains lead.

Because of its size and shape, cazuelas are ideal for making a wide variety of dishes such as stews, casserole-style dishes, and capirotada, a bread pudding. It is also the preferred dish for making traditional mole, which is a well-known dish from the Puebla area consisting of over thirty ingredients.

Cazuela

- A cazuela is a very useful piece of cookware that can be used to create many dishes, so you may want to have more than one on hand for making multiple dishes at one time.

- Cazuelas get better the more you use them, so be sure to use yours often.

- Some staining and discoloration of the interior is a normal part of the seasoning process, so don't try to scrub off every last bit of evidence that it was used.

Using the Cazuela in the Oven

- A cazuela can easily replace most glass or metal baking dishes.

- A well-seasoned cazuela adds a signature flavor to the items you cook in it, as it absorbs a small amount

- of flavor from each previous dish that was cooked in it.

- It can take years of regular use to create a beautifully seasoned surface that is naturally nonstick and low maintenance.

If you are going to use a cazuela on a stove top, electric or gas, you will need to use a diffuser under the cazuela, which will help distribute the heat and prevent scorching. And since earthenware is very sensitive to sudden temperature changes, you should place the food into the cazuela and let it warm up very slowly over low heat. As it warms, you can adjust the heat as called for by the recipe you are using.

ZOOM

Unglazed earthenware is very porous. When you make a recipe in your cazuela, many of the flavors and seasonings will absorb into the clay. If you cook a strongly flavored item and it becomes overpowering, clean your cazuela by soaking it and rubbing it with baking soda. For a regular cleaning, soak it and rub it with a towel. Do not use soap on your cazuela because it may also be absorbed.

A Cazuela on the Stove Top with a Diffuser

- While cazuelas are perfect for baked dishes, they can also be successfully used on the stove top.

- To prevent damaging the pot or scorching the contents, always use a diffuser, which sits over the heating element (gas or electric) so that the cazuela does not come into direct contact with the heat source.

- Do not begin heating the pot until the contents are in place. Bring the heat up very slowly, over the course of 5 to 10 minutes, starting with the lowest setting.

Caring for Your Cazuela

- Before you use your cazuela for the first time, soak it in water for about 30 minutes and then rub it dry.

- Soak any unglazed portions of the cazuela for twenty minutes before use.

- After cooking in your cazuela, simply wipe out any remaining food or soak it to soften any stubborn bits.

- Remember that some staining and discoloration is normal.

BEANS

Beans are a native and nutritional ingredient often served as a side dish

Beans were one of the first staple crops in early Mexico. The Mexican Indians survived on beans because they are high in fiber, protein, and nutrients. They were often seasoned with chiles, another native ingredient, to give them more flavor.

There are many varieties of beans, but one of the most popular bean types in northern Mexico is the pinto bean. These medium-size beans are light brown with darker brown speckles. They become a more solid brown when cooked, and they have a somewhat grainy texture. Pinto beans are the bean of choice for a common side dish called refried beans and are called "pintos" when the beans are served whole.

In the southern states of Mexico, the black bean is the most common bean. Small in size with a mild, earthy flavor, black

Pinto Beans

- Beans are very easy to find in almost any location. You can find them in your grocery store in ready-to-go bags, and they are sometimes found loose in bins that you scoop out yourself.

- Beans can retain their freshness for up to a year. Beans older than that should be discarded.

- A few shriveled or bad beans are normal; you can discard them. But overall they should be uniform in size and color.

Black Beans

- Beans will absorb a significant amount of water while soaking, so make sure there is plenty of water. It is better to have too much, than too little.

- After soaking, the water may become cloudy or have a few bubbles in it. This is normal.

- If you leave your beans for too long, and they begin to have a significantly bad odor, discard them. A usual overnight soaking will not cause this, but if you leave them for the day as well, it could become a problem.

beans are usually left whole when cooking and are often served in the cooking liquid.

Beans are widely available in dried and canned form. Dried beans are preferable in most dishes so they can absorb some of the flavors of what they are cooked in. However, they can take 6 to 8 hours to cook. Canned beans are a quicker alternative, but they do not taste as good and tend to have a mushier texture.

ZOOM

If you cook with dried beans, you must first sort through them, as they often have a few small pebbles or other debris mixed in. After you remove the debris, place the beans in a bowl and cover with water. Let them sit out overnight or for at least 8 hours. They will absorb some of the water but still be firm to the touch. They will then be ready for use.

Cooking Beans

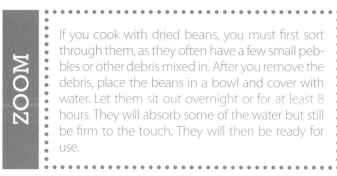

- Beans absorb the flavors from the liquids they are cooked in, so make sure to use drinking water or broth to cook them in.

- Beans can be cooked in a metal cooking pot, an earthenware olla, or even in a pressure cooker. As long as they have adequate cooking time to absorb liquid and soften, you can cook them in whatever you like.

Serving the Beans

- Beans can be used in recipes or enjoyed alone. They are often served by the ladle with the cooking liquid, which forms a thickened broth during cooking.

- Beans can also be used in soups, stews, or even salads. They are a common ingredient in burritos and on tostadas.

RICE

This versatile grain is a popular side dish as well as an ingredient in other dishes

There is some debate about how and when rice was introduced into Mexican cuisine, but over the last 400 years it has become a staple in the Mexican diet. It can be served plain or as a simple side dish or used as a base for main dishes with many ingredients. Rice is also used as an ingredient for burritos and helps absorb juices from the contents that could

make the tortilla soggy. There are a couple of types of rice usually used in Mexican recipes. The first one is long-grain white rice. It has a drier, fluffier texture and is good for making Mexican rice and other rice side dishes. In Mexico the germ may be left on the rice, which looks like a black speck at the tip of each grain. The germ does not really make a difference

Long-Grain Rice

- Long-grain rice is easy to find in your local grocery store.

- It is fairly easy to work with, but it can become mushy quickly when it is overcooked.

- Make sure to taste a grain or two before you remove it from the heat to make sure it has cooked through and is not hard or crunchy.

- Long-grain rice is best served fresh, as it becomes dry and stiff when refrigerated and then reheated.

Mexican Rice

- Long-grain rice is a great choice for side dishes such as Mexican rice because the grains stay separate and fluffy, allowing for a nice coating of flavorings on each individual grain.

- Long-grain rice can be rinsed before cooking Mexi-

can rice to help the grains stay fluffy.

- When cooking Mexican rice the liquids are absorbed into the grains and the steam helps to cook it. To keep the steam inside, do not remove the lid for more than a few seconds.

in how the rice cooks or tastes.

Another type of rice used is medium-grain rice, which has a slightly smaller, rounder grain. Medium-grain rice has a much stickier consistency than long-grain rice and a creamy texture when it is cooked. Because of its texture it lends itself well to rice puddings and in recipes in which the rice is not the main ingredient, such as soups.

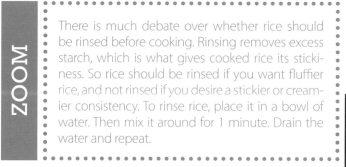

ZOOM

There is much debate over whether rice should be rinsed before cooking. Rinsing removes excess starch, which is what gives cooked rice its stickiness. So rice should be rinsed if you want fluffier rice, and not rinsed if you desire a stickier or creamier consistency. To rinse rice, place it in a bowl of water. Then mix it around for 1 minute. Drain the water and repeat.

Medium-Grain Rice

- Medium-grain rice is usually found near the long-grain rice, and you can substitute short-grain rice if necessary.

- Medium-grain rice is a little bit easier and more forgiving to work with than long grain. Even if it is slightly overcooked, it is not as noticeable because of its naturally stickier texture.

- For a less sticky, yet chewier rice dish, use medium-grain rice, but rinse it before using to help remove excess starch.

Arroz Con Leche—Rice Pudding

- For a dish that has a creamy or sticky texture, do not rinse the rice prior to cooking with it. The starch will help create the desired texture in the final dish.

- Begin checking the texture of the rice a minute or two before the end of the suggested cooking time in case it has cooked more quickly and needs to be removed from the heat.

- When the rice is done, there is no need to fluff it because of the sticky quality.

DRIED & CANNED CHILES

Chiles are essential to many authentic sauces, marinades, and traditional Mexican dishes

Chiles are a must-have in any Mexican kitchen. Recipes often call for dried chiles, but canned varieties are a suitable source if fresh are not available.

Dried chiles are very useful because they have a long shelf life, are easy to prepare, and add delicious flavor to recipes. You can find dried chiles in the Latin section of your grocery store, or you can order them online. Look for chiles that are whole (not broken or torn) and have a nice uniform color (not mottled or streaked). Depending on the type of chile, they can range in color from deep red to dark brown. Some commonly used dried chiles are ancho, guajillo, and pasilla. Dried chiles are usually rehydrated and blended before use.

Dried Red Chiles

- Red chiles are often strung together on a rope to make *ristas*, which can be hung in the kitchen to allow the chiles to dry out and easy to access.

- You can also find dried chiles at many major gro-

cery store chains in plastic cellophane bags near the other Mexican herbs and spices.

- Another option is to order them online. Dried chiles can last over a year, so make sure to stock up.

Canned Green Chiles

- Green chile season is considered to be late summer through fall, when most of the chiles planted in spring have matured and are ready to be harvested.

- Green chiles do fairly well and retain their color and flavor when canned. Although they are not

quite as flavorful as fresh green chiles, their canned substitutes are pretty close in flavor and texture.

- Green chiles are roasted and peeled before use. They are often seeded and then stuffed with cheese or a meat filling, or they are diced and used as a flavoring.

If you do not have access to fresh chiles or if green chiles are out of season, you can use canned versions. Canned roasted green chiles (diced or whole) and jalapeños are easily found in the Latin section of your grocery store or ordered online. Another great canned chile to have on hand is chipotle in adobo sauce. These spicy-hot chiles are used with the canning sauce to add a smoky flavor to recipes.

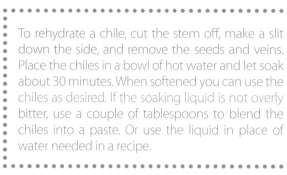

ZOOM

To rehydrate a chile, cut the stem off, make a slit down the side, and remove the seeds and veins. Place the chiles in a bowl of hot water and let soak about 30 minutes. When softened you can use the chiles as desired. If the soaking liquid is not overly bitter, use a couple of tablespoons to blend the chiles into a paste. Or use the liquid in place of water needed in a recipe.

Pickled Jalapeños

- Chiles, mainly jalapeños, are often pickled. The pickled versions are usually used in recipes, but they can also be used as a condiment.

- Pickled jalapeños have a very strong jalapeño flavor that is often desired in jalapeño-flavored recipes.

- Jalapeños are often pickled with other vegetables such as onions or carrots.

Chipotle Chiles in Adobo Sauce

- Smoked and dried jalapeños are called chipotle chiles. You can find them in their dried form, but they are also found canned in adobo sauce.

- The adobo sauce absorbs the smokiness and heat of the chipotles, and many recipes call for the use of the sauce as well as the chipotles.

SEASONINGS

Traditional herbs and spices are the key to many authentic Mexican recipes

The seasonings are what give Mexican food its signature flavor. A common flavor combination is ground chiles, cumin, garlic, and oregano. Another signature Mexican flavoring is achiote, made from annatto seeds. You will find these spices individually incorporated into a dish, or combined in varying amounts to create a uniquely Mexican taste.

Before the Spanish invaded Mexico and began to influence the native cuisine, the Aztecs seasoned their dishes with chiles of varying flavors and heat intensities. Salt was also a major seasoning, as well as achiote, epazote, honey, hoja santa leaves, and cocoa. All of these seasonings and flavorings still play a key part in modern Mexican cuisine.

Ground Red Chiles

- One spice commonly used is ground chile, which is simply a dried chile that has been ground up.

- The label will indicate the type of chile used and the heat level and flavor of the spice.

- A more common version, north of the border, is called "chili powder," which contains small amounts of dried onion, garlic, and oregano.

- You can cook with ground chile and chili powder or sprinkle them on after cooking.

Cumin, Whole and Ground

- Another signature flavor of many Mexican dishes comes from cumin, an earthy flavored spice.

- Cumin has a very bold and strong smoky flavor and can be used in its ground or seed form.

- Cumin pairs especially well with chicken dishes and ground beef and is occasionally used in soups and stews.

With the introduction of European ingredients and spices, Mexican food began to transform into a melting pot of flavors. The Mayans and Aztecs added the new seasonings to their traditional recipes to add new zest to old stand-bys.

ZOOM

You can easily find ground chile, cumin, and oregano in the spices aisle of most grocery stores. For a more authentic approach, find Mexican brands of spices in the Latin section of your store. Often they will be packaged in plastic bags and are less expensive. You can just refill your current spice jars with the contents of the bags, or put the contents into an airtight bag after opening.

Mexican Oregano

- Mexican oregano is another seasoning widely used throughout Mexico. It contains the same oils as Mediterranean oregano, but it's a different species.

- Mexican oregano leaves curl up when dried, so this seasoning is also known as curly-leaf oregano.

- Mexican oregano has a grassy aroma and is often used in combination with cumin and ground chile.

- Mediterranean oregano is an acceptable substitute if the Mexican version is not available.

A Selection of Mexican Spices

- Mexican herbs and spices are often found in cellophane bags along with dried chiles and tamarind.

- Once the bag is opened, storage becomes an issue.

- You can simply place the unused portions into separate airtight plastic bags or invest in small glass spice jars that you can refill with the bagged spices.

BREADS & FLOURS

Homemade tortillas and freshly baked breads are an integral part of Mexican cuisine

Two types of flours are used in Mexican cooking. The most widely used is masa harina, which is used for corn tortillas, tamales, and sopes. Masa harina is easily found in the Latin section of your grocery store or can be ordered online. It is off white and easily used by adding water and sometimes lard and seasonings to create a dough. Masa harina is also a

delicious ingredient in many hot beverages, helping thicken them.

Another common variety of flour is wheat flour, which was brought into Mexico by the Spaniards and further processed into white flour. White flour is primarily used for flour tortillas, white breads, cakes, and cookies and can be found in the

Masa Harina

- *Masa harina* means "dough flour."

- Masa harina is made in several steps. First the corn is processed to remove the hull and germ. Then the corn is ground to form masa, or dough. The masa

- is then dried and ground again to create masa harina.

- Fresh masa is great to use if you have access to it, but masa harina is a perfectly acceptable substitute.

Fresh Corn Tortillas

- In Mexico the primary use of masa harina and white flour is to make tortillas.

- Tortillas are served at almost every meal, whether eaten as a side dish or as part of the main dish.

- White flour tortillas are more common in Northern Mexico, while corn tortillas are preferred in the south.

- Tortillerias are shops that focus entirely on making tortillas. Buy enough to last you one or two days, then go back for more.

baking section of your grocery store.

In Mexico, breads are usually bought at a *panaderia* (bakery) and are always baked fresh every day using no preservatives, so the bread needs to be used within a couple of days. The name for bread is *pan* and each variety is named for its shape. For example, conchas are named for their shell shape and cuernos for their horn shape. Another is *pan dulce,* which is bread that is slightly sweet with a decorative topping.

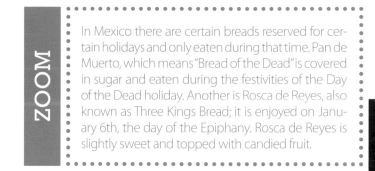

ZOOM

In Mexico there are certain breads reserved for certain holidays and only eaten during that time. Pan de Muerto, which means "Bread of the Dead" is covered in sugar and eaten during the festivities of the Day of the Dead holiday. Another is Rosca de Reyes, also known as Three Kings Bread; it is enjoyed on January 6th, the day of the Epiphany. Rosca de Reyes is slightly sweet and topped with candied fruit.

Freshly Baked Bolillos

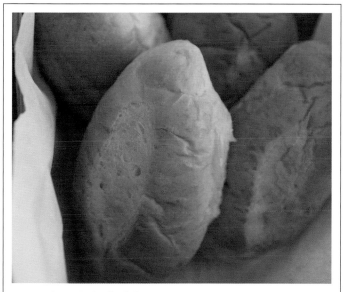

- Panaderias bake fresh bread on a daily basis and display it on trays in their windows.

- *Bolillos* are a popular type of bread used to make Mexican sandwiches called *tortas*.

- Mexican bread bought at a panaderia should be consumed within two or three days, as they contain no preservatives.

Pan Dulce—Mexican Sweet Bread

- Pan dulce, or sweet bread, is another very popular bakery item. The bread itself is slightly sweet, and the colorful, decorative topping adds even more sweetness.

- Pan dulce comes in many designs and colors, which are purely eye-catching. The bread and toppings are not flavored to match the colors.

- Even though the designs may look difficult, it is easy to carve a design into the topping with a knife.

SWEETS

These sweeteners are used to add flavor and dimension to traditional Mexican dishes

While refined white sugar is now used throughout Mexico as a sweetener, there are a few traditional sweeteners that are called for in many authentic Mexican recipes.

One sweetener is *piloncillo*, an unrefined sugar made from sugarcane juice that has a rich molasses flavor even though it contains none. It can be light or dark brown in color and is sold by the ounce in small-, medium-, and large-size cones. Piloncillo is very hard; you need to break it up into smaller pieces before using it, and when stored in a cool, dry place, it will last virtually forever. You can find piloncillo in the Latin section of your grocery store near the chiles and spices, or you can order it online.

Piloncillo Cone

- Piloncillo is measured in ounces rather than spoons or cups.

- Piloncillo is named for its conical shape and means "pylon."

- Unlike white sugar, piloncillo is unrefined and minimally processed.

- Piloncillo is the sweetener of choice when sugar is called for in a Mexican recipe.

Breaking Up the Piloncillo for Use

- Piloncillo has a very hard texture and needs to be broken up into pieces before use.

- A serrated knife is ideal for this job, because piloncillo is so hard that a straight knife might slide off the surface.

- If the Piloncillo is too hard, microwave it for 20 seconds at a time to soften it.

- Even though the flavor is compared to brown sugar, piloncillo also has maple flavors.

Mexican chocolate has a long history in Mexico, and its flavor is very different from other chocolate. It is dark and flavored with cinnamon and occasionally other spices, or sometimes chiles are added. Mexican chocolate can be eaten plain or used to make hot beverages, desserts, and sauces.

Honey is another sweetener used to add flavor to dishes such as candied pumpkin or as a topping or dip for pastries.

········· GREEN ● LIGHT ·········
While using authentic ingredients gives you the best and most flavorful results, there are substitutions you can use in a pinch. For each 8 ounces of piloncillo called for in a recipe you can substitute 1 cup of loosely packed brown sugar and 1 tablespoon of molasses. If you don't have Mexican chocolate on hand, substitute dark chocolate and a pinch of cinnamon for each ounce.

Mexican Chocolate

- Mexican chocolate comes in disks or tablets that make it easy to measure.

- Each disk or tablet is divided into wedges which can be broken off for measuring.

- Tablets of Mexican chocolate are primarily used for cooking and baking.

- Mexican chocolate has a somewhat grainy texture and yet is smooth due to the cocoa butter.

Mexican Honey

- Honey was used by the Aztecs and Mayans to add flavor and sweetness to recipes.

- In Mexico you can find honey sold by the jar and also in plastic straws. The straws are intended to be enjoyed like candy; just snip the end and sip the contents.

- Honey is still used as a sweetener as well as a flavoring for many dishes. It is also used as a topping and a dip.

FRESH CHILES

From mild to hot, chiles can be found in almost every Mexican dish

Chiles were first cultivated in the days of the ancient Aztec Indians, when they were used to flavor their diet of corn and beans. In modern dishes they are not only used as a seasoning, they are also stuffed and served as a main dish.

Chiles come in many shapes and sizes and there are over one hundred varieties from the mild Sweet Bell to the fiery habanero. It is best to wear gloves when handling very hot chiles, as the oils could burn your skin.

The heat from the chile comes from a substance called capsaicin that is found in the flesh and concentrated in the seeds and the white veins that run inside the chile. Removing them will remove some of the heat.

The difference between green and red chiles is simply that red chiles are fully ripened and tend to be hotter. Different

Small Green Chiles

- Jalapeños are small green chiles that are quite hot.

- They are often pickled or canned, and different recipes call for different jalapeño preparations.

- Serrano chiles are quite a bit hotter than jalapeños and are a bit smaller in size. Depending on the heat level you wish, they can pretty much be used interchangeably.

Small Red Chiles

- Red chiles come in many sizes and shapes. When they are dried, they can take on a wrinkled appearance or may maintain a smooth skin.

- Dried Red chiles are often ground into a powder for seasoning.

- Fresh red chiles can also be sewn together to create a *ristra* or wreath of chiles. The fresh chiles dry out while on the wreath, and you can remove them and use them all year long.

names are given to chiles depending on the degree of ripeness and any other preparations. For example a poblano is a dark green fresh chile, but when it is ripened and dried it becomes an ancho chile. The jalapeño is a fresh green or red chile that becomes a chipotle when it is smoked and dried.

ZOOM

Most recipes call for roasted chiles. When you roast a chile, you char it and remove the skins, adding flavor. You can roast a chile over an open flame, on a comal, in a broiler, or on a grill. Char until the skin is black and blistered. Then place the chile in a plastic bag or covered bowl for a few minutes. The skin will be easy to peel off and the seeds and veins can be scraped out.

Roasted Green Chiles

- Green chiles are roasted before they are used in recipes.

- To roast a chile they need to be cook over a fire or broiled until the skins turn black.

- Even though the skins are removed prior to use, the roasting process cooks the chile and adds a delicious smoky flavor.

- Green chiles come in many shapes and sizes, from the long, narrow, light green Anaheim chile to the dark green, stout poblano.

Removing the Seeds

- Chiles range in heat from sweet and mild to pungent and fiery.

- The capsaicin is concentrated in the white veins of the chile, which hold the seeds. If you scrape out the veins, you can reduce the amount of heat.

- The white, pithy veins can be easily scraped out with a spoon and discarded.

- In most chile recipes the stem, veins, and seeds are discarded.

ONIONS & GARLIC

Onions and garlic are absolute necessities for flavoring authentic Mexican dishes

Although they are somewhat low in nutrition, onions are an integral part of the Mexican diet. They are primarily used as a flavoring and are essential to many Mexican recipes. They can be raw or cooked and used in a recipe, or freshly chopped and used as a topping.

Both onions and garlic are in the lily family, and each has

its own unique flavor. They are primarily used as a seasoning and cooked as an ingredient of a final dish. Even though they are often used together in recipes, garlic is not used raw as a topping as onions are.

Onions and garlic are best when fresh. You can easily find them in the produce section of the grocery store or at a local

Onions

- Large onions are easier to work with and cut than smaller ones.

- Cut off only the portion you will need and leave the skin on the remaining portion. The skin will help it stay fresher longer.

- Cut onions are so powerful, they can give everything in the refrigerator an onion flavor. To avoid this, store cut onions in glass jars or several layers of plastic bags.

- Soak an onion in cool water for a few minutes to make it easier to peel.

Garlic

- A single clove of garlic is three times stronger if pressed through a garlic press than if chopped or diced.

- Sometimes a garlic clove will sprout; this is normal. Use it immediately and discard the sprouted areas.

- Easily loosen the skin from a garlic clove by cutting the ends off, then place the flat side of a knife on top of the clove. Hold the knife with one hand, and carefully bring the palm of your other hand firmly down onto the knife. The clove will break open.

farmers' market. Check them to make sure they are not soft or have soft areas. They should be firm with intact skins and no large tears or mold around the root area.

A whole onion or bulb of garlic needs no refrigeration. Onions will be fine for three to four weeks and a garlic bulb for three to four months if kept in a cool, dry area. However once it is cut or the outer papery skin broken, you need to refrigerate it until you are ready to use it.

ZOOM

While fresh onions and garlic are ideal choices there are alternatives. Crushed or chopped garlic can be found jarred. Use $1/2$ teaspoon for each clove garlic called for in your recipe. Substitute $1/4$ teaspoon garlic powder (not garlic salt) for each clove. Use 1 tablespoon onion powder to replace an entire onion. Powders are not precooked and need to be added with the other ingredients.

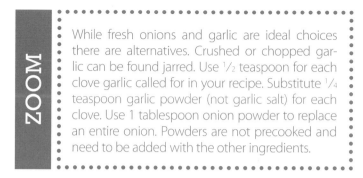

Sautéing Onions and Garlic

- Onions and garlic are sometimes referred to as aromatics.

- They are often cooked together as the start to many soups, rice dishes, and more.

- Onions have a longer cooking time, so begin cooking them first and add the garlic in the last few minutes, as it can burn quickly.

- Use medium heat to cook onions and garlic to allow them to soften and become golden. High heat can burn garlic.

Onions and Cilantro

- Raw onions are usually used as a topping for tacos, soups, and stews.

- Onions are usually chopped very finely when used as a topping.

- The root end is the area that is thought to contain the juices that cause your eyes to burn, so cut the top portion off first in order to peel the skin back.

FRESH INGREDIENTS

TOMATOES

These delicious fruits add color and flavor to many Mexican dishes

Tomatoes are native to Central and South America, just south of Mexico. It is unclear just how they migrated north into Mexico, but they have been used in Mexican cooking for hundreds of years.

Tomatoes come in many varieties, but if a Mexican recipe is unspecific, then Roma tomatoes are a good choice. Plum tomatoes have a nice, firm flesh with little seeds or juice.

Because they have less juice, they won't water down your dish.

Standard slicing tomatoes (beefsteak, round, or globe) are rounder and juicier and can also be used when tomatoes are called for, but some of the seeds and juices may add additional liquid to the dish you are preparing.

Fresh tomatoes are the base of many authentic dishes such

Heirloom Varieties

- Roma tomatoes are a type of plum tomato. They have few seeds and thick flesh, which make them ideal for canning and storage.

- They are an egg shape and are sometimes yellow.

- Other, larger tomato varieties have more seeds and, depending on the variety, can have more flavorful flesh.

- While the seeds do add some flavor, they are very watery and can make dishes watery, so you may need to discard the seeds.

Vine Ripened Tomatoes

- Fresh-picked tomatoes are the best choice, as they have ripened on the vine and have superior texture and flavor to a tomato bought at the market.

- If you cannot grow them yourself, you can find fresh-picked tomatoes at most farmers' markets.

- If buying at the market, look for tomatoes that are still attached to the vine.

- Refrigerated tomatoes quickly lose their flavor, so store them in a cool, dry place.

as salsas and sauces. They add a fresh, tangy flavor and a beautiful red color to each dish they are used in.

Since tomatoes are easily grown in many climates, they are readily available in most areas. Look for tomatoes that are brightly colored and heavy for their size. Hothouse tomatoes and tomatoes with some of the vine still attached are usually more flavorful.

······· GREEN ● LIGHT ·············

Fully ripened tomatoes fresh off the vine have much more flavor than their store-bought counterparts. Since they grow well in most regions, you can easily grow tomatoes in your backyard. Although they do not do well in winter, you can either regrow them in spring or bring them in the house for winter. They yield less fruit during extremely hot summer conditions. Find supplies at your local hardware store, gardening center, or nursery.

Cooking Tomatoes

- Tomatoes are delicious fresh and can be cooked as well. The soft tomato flesh becomes a delicious sauce when cooked slowly over medium or low heat.

- Many sauces in Mexican cooking are tomato based and often include onions or garlic.

- Large, juicy tomatoes make good candidates for a delicious sauce.

Using Tomatoes for Salsa

- Fresh tomatoes are often chopped up with onions, garlic, and cilantro to make a condiment known as salsa Mexicana or *pico de gallo*.

- They are also pureed with other ingredients such as fresh green chiles, jalape-ños, onions, or garlic to create different types of salsa.

- The fresher and more ripe the tomatoes are, the better your salsa will taste, so be sure to use the best tomatoes you can find.

FRESH INGREDIENTS

TOMATILLOS
Just a few tangy tomatillos can add immense flavor to a dish

Tomatillos are a distant relative of the tomato, but they have very few similarities. Tomatillos are green, have a sticky residue on their skin, and are covered by a papery husk that you remove before use.

A tomatillo that is perfectly ripe has light green and white flesh with small seeds. It is very tart and has a young, grassy flavor.

Tomatillos are used in salsa verde (green salsa) and chile verde (green chile stew) to give them their signature, tart flavors. A little goes a long way, so use them sparingly.

Most large grocery stores or Latin markets have an abundant supply of tomatillos. Tomatillos are small in size, ranging from a cherry tomato to a golf ball. The smaller tomatillos are sweeter. Look for ones that are firm to the touch and have

Whole Tomatillos

- Tomatillos should be stored in a cool, dry place in the open air. They should not be stored in an airtight container.

- They should be stored with the husks on until you are ready to use or freeze them.

- The condition of the husk is a good indication of the fruit, so make sure the husk is intact and free of shriveled, moldy, or discolored areas.

Removing the Husks

- The husk is inedible and must be removed and discarded before eating or processing the fruit.

- The husk is easily peeled off with your fingers. Gently tear the husk and then pull it back in pieces until the fruit is fully exposed.

- The tomatillo should fill out the husk, and the fruit should be touching the husk but not bursting through it.

tightly closed husks. The husk should be a uniform green color with no yellowing. If a tomatillo is beginning to yellow, it is too ripe and should be discarded.

ZOOM

Tomatillos in their husks can be placed in a paper bag and left in a cool, dry area for a week or two, or refrigerated up to four weeks. For long-term storage, remove them from their husks, rinse and dry them, and then freeze them in an airtight plastic freezer bag. When you want to use them, pull out as many as you like, let them thaw, and cook as usual.

Inside of a Tomatillo

- The inside of a tomatillo is much different from a tomato. The flesh is firm and white, and the seeds are very small and embedded in the flesh.

- The flesh should be wet and have plenty of moisture.

- When a recipe calls for tomatillos, the entire fruit is used, including the skin, flesh, and seeds.

- Rinse off the sticky residue before using tomatillos in a recipe.

Using Tomatillos to Make Salsa

- Tomatillos can vary in flavor from very tart to mild and somewhat sweet. The flavor will have a direct impact on the final dish.

- If a sweeter tomatillo is necessary but only very tart ones are available, you can add a pinch of sugar for each tomatillo used to balance the tartness.

- Tomatillos are often used raw in Mexican sauces, but they can also be roasted or cooked as part of a recipe.

PLANTAINS

This starchy tropical fruit is used in main dishes and desserts throughout Mexico

Plantains are grown in tropical locations and used throughout Mexico, especially in the tropical Yucatan Peninsula region. They originate from Asia but are now grown in almost every tropical climate.

Plantains are in the banana family but are very different from the yellow bananas that are eaten raw. Plantains are very starchy and sometimes used in their green unripened state in baked or boiled dishes, but they are more often used in their sweeter, ripened state.

When a plantain is ripening, it starts out bright green and very hard. The inside of an unripe plantain has a mild flavor and no sweetness. As it ripens it begins to yellow and

KNACK MEXICAN COOKING

Plantains

- Plantains look just like a traditional banana, but they are about twice the size and much firmer to the touch.

- They often have dark spots and small marks, which are normal.

- Green plantains have very little flavor and can be cooked similarly to potatoes.

- Yellow plantains are the most versatile, as they have begun to ripen and develop a little bit of flavor and sweetness.

Preparing to Remove the Peel

- Plantains are available all year long and can be found at most local grocery stores or at Mexican or Latin American grocers. You can also ask the produce manager to order them.

- The peel of a plantain is very tough and difficult to remove.

- The easiest way to peel a plantain is to cut off the ends and cut the rest into three pieces. Use a knife to score through the flesh three or four times down each piece.

becomes slightly softer. At this stage it can still be used for baking or stuffing. When it has fully blackened, it develops a sweeter taste (still not as sweet as a yellow banana) and is often baked and used for desserts.

Plantain leaves are also used in Mexican cooking for wrapping meat to create a steaming effect. The leaves keep the meat tender and moist as well as incorporate a unique flavor to the dish.

MAKE IT EASY

To peel a green or yellow plantain, cut the ends off and cut the plantain into two or three pieces. Then score the peel, cutting it as deep as the skin itself. Make about six scores down the length of the plantain, which allows you to peel the pieces off. Black plantains can be peeled like a yellow banana. Continue to pull the peel off by strips.

Removing the Peel

- After you have scored the flesh, you can lift it or peel it off of the plantain. If the skin is very difficult, you may need to score it a few more times.

- The skin should be peeled crosswise against the fruit, not downward as in a traditional banana.

- You can store peeled plantains submerged in water in the refrigerator for up to three days.

- You can also store peeled plantains in an airtight container in the freezer for up to three months.

Blackened Plantain

- If you purchase a plantain that is already blackened, make sure it is still slightly firm to the touch and not mushy or moldy.

- Plantains should keep their shape when cooked.

If it is too mushy, it is over ripe and won't hold up to cooking.

- You can bake a ripened plantain in its skin just like a potato.

FRESH INGREDIENTS

FRESH HERBS

Fresh herbs and spices add a fresh flavor to the dishes prepared with them

Herbs have played a major role in the signature flavors of well-known Mexican dishes. While many of these herbs are regionally available in Mexico, they can be hard to find elsewhere. However, there are still a few that are easily found at your local grocery store, such as cilantro and oregano. With the use of fresh herbs becoming more popular, the variety of

herbs available continues to increase.

While there were many indigenous herbs already used by the native Mexicans, many new herbs were introduced by the Spaniards. These added a European and Asian flair to traditional dishes. Mexican cooking continues to evolve with the use of local ingredients and regional dishes combined

Cilantro

- Cilantro is a very pungent herb that resembles flat-leaf parsley. Check the tag to make sure you get the right one.

- If you are familiar with cilantro, you can tell just by the smell that you have the right one.

- It has a unique citrus flavor that is somewhat bitter and tangy, and some people claim it tastes of soap.

- Fresh cilantro is easily found in most grocery stores, usually near the parsley. Look for it to be bright green with no yellowing or brown spots.

Epazote

- Epazote is a classic Mexican herb used primarily for seasoning beans, but it can be used in other dishes.

- It is poisonous in large quantities, and that may have prevented it from gaining popularity north of the border.

- Epazote is harmless in the amounts used to cook with.

- It has long pointy leaves that may appear somewhat wilted, and it can easily be found in a Mexican market.

with new flavors that sometimes have an Asian, Caribbean, or European influence.

Herbs such as chaya, hoja santa, papalo, chepiche, and chepilin are all classic Mexican herbs that flavor classic and traditional dishes. The Spanish introduced new herbs such as thyme, parsley, marjoram, and cilantro, which were infused into local dishes. Cilantro has become very popular. It complements many native Mexican ingredients and is a signature flavor in modern Mexican cooking.

··········· GREEN●LIGHT ·············

Although herbs and seasoning can be found at the market, it is handy to have a fresh supply in your own garden, especially for herbs that are more difficult to find. You can easily plant herbs in a small pot and keep it in a window with plenty of sunlight. There are even special herb-growing appliances that provide light and perfect growing conditions year-round.

FRESH INGREDIENTS

Oregano

- Mexican oregano is related to verbena, but it contains the same oils that give Mediterranean oregano its flavor.

- Mexican oregano is slightly stronger in flavor than the Mediterranean version, so less is needed.

- Since fresh oregano has a milder flavor, you can use about ¼ cup of fresh leaves for every tablespoon of dried oregano called for in a recipe.

- Mexican oregano is sometimes used as a substitute for epazote.

Fresh Herbs

- Fresh herbs have a much milder flavor than their dried versions, so you will need to use three or four times as much fresh herbs as you would dried.

- Fresh herbs can be kept in the refrigerator in a glass of water, similar to flowers. Place a plastic bag loosely over the top.

- You can freeze herbs into ice cubes. Simply toss a few cubes into soups or defrost and drain before use.

SOPES

These little masa cakes make a delicious snack or appetizer

Sopes are delicious, handmade fried cakes of masa harina that are considered an *antojito*, or finger food. The cakes are made fresh and then piled high with your favorite toppings such as beans, meats, onions, and cheese. The sopes cakes have a slight ridge around the outside, which helps keep the toppings from sliding off.

Sopes are similar to a garnacha, which is a street food made with a small fried tortilla topped with meat, onions, and pickled cabbage. Garnachas are a popular street food in the Mexican city of Oaxaca.

Sopes are easy to make, and even the most novice cook should be able to prepare them with ease. Like most antojitos, sopes are best eaten fresh off the comal. *Yield: Serves 6*

Sopes

Ingredients

1 1/2 cups masa harina

1/2 cup white flour

1 teaspoon salt

1 1/2 cups water

3 tablespoons cooking oil

1 cup refried beans

1 cup shredded beef

1/2 cup crumbled Cotija cheese

- Combine the masa harina, white flour, and salt in a large bowl. Add the water and stir until a soft dough forms.

- Use your hands to create the masa cake. Heat the oil on a medium-hot comal. Cook the cake in oil for a couple of minutes on each side.

- Let each sope cool briefly before creating a ridge. Return to the comal to finish cooking, 1 to 2 minutes.

- Remove sope from comal and top with equal layers beans, shredded beef, and cheese.

Grilled Chicken Sopes: You can top sopes with any of your favorite meats. Try using some mashed black beans as the base (you can easily mash them with a bit of their liquid with the back of a fork). After you spread on the beans, add a few strips of freshly grilled chicken. Top the chicken with a generous spoonful of your favorite spicy salsa. For the final touch add a sprinkle of Cotija cheese.

Vegetarian Sopes: Use your favorite vegetarian toppings too. Spread a layer of refried beans over the sope cake. Top the beans with a hearty helping of freshly grilled sliced onions that are just beginning to brown and a couple of slices of grilled red bell peppers. Add a pinch of chopped cilantro and a sprinkle of Cotija.

Creating the Sope Cake

Topping the Sopes

- Separate the dough into walnut-size portions. Roll each into a smooth ball.

- Press each ball into a 3-inch patty about ¼-inch thick. You can do this between your palms or use a rolling pin.

- Heat the oil on a comal over medium heat and cook sopes 2 minutes each side. Let them cool to the touch and, using your fingers, pinch the edges up to create a ridge.

- Return sopes to hot oil and cook 1 minute on each side.

- Have the toppings warm and ready. You can make them beforehand and reheat them as you make the sopes.

- Spread a thin layer of refried beans over the sope.

- Add about ⅛ cup shredded beef to the top of the beans. Press down a little to make sure the beef sticks to the beans.

- Sprinkle a generous amount of Cotija over the top and serve immediately.

APPETIZERS & SNACKS

PICO DE GALLO

This is a popular blend of chopped tomatoes, onions, cilantro, and chiles

Pico de gallo is a popular salsa and is commonly served as an appetizer. In Mexico it is known as salsa Mexicana. The difference between pico de gallo and other salsas is that it is chunky and somewhat dry. For a quick and easy snack, serve up some fresh pico de gallo with your favorite tortilla chips. This fresh and delicious salsa also makes a great topping for tacos, grilled chicken, and fish. It has a mild heat from the small amount of jalapeño added to the dish.

Pico de gallo's flavor depends on the freshness of the ingredients. When ripe and fresh ingredients are used, the flavors are well rounded and balanced. You can adjust the amount of jalapeño to add more heat. *Yield: Serves 8*

Ingredients

6 Roma or plum tomatoes

¹/₂ medium white onion

1 jalapeño

5 cloves garlic

1 handful cilantro leaves

2 tablespoons fresh lime juice

¹/₂ teaspoon salt

Pico de Gallo

- Dice the tomatoes, discarding the majority of the seeds and juice. Add them to a large bowl.

- Chop the onion and add it to the tomatoes. Seed and dice the jalapeño and add it to the bowl.

- After removing the garlic skins, chop the garlic and cilantro, and add them to the bowl.

- Sprinkle with lime juice and salt, toss ingredients to combine.

MAKE IT YOUR OWN

The great thing about pico de gallo is that it is a very versatile recipe. If you like a spicier version, double the amount of jalapeño or use a serrano chile instead. Or try using a red onion for a slightly different flavor and some added color. Lemon juice or white vinegar can be used in place of the lime juice for another tasty version. Also try adding more cilantro for some added zing.

GREEN ● LIGHT

Fresh and flavorful ingredients are the keys to delicious Pico de Gallo. If you use bland or old produce, your finished product will lack flavor and color. Purchase your ingredients no more than two to three days before you make the recipe so that they are as fresh as possible. To bring out even more flavor, let Pico de Gallo rest in the refrigerator for about an hour.

Removing the Seeds

- To make sure the Pico de Gallo is not watery, remove some of the seeds from the tomatoes.

- Slice a small amount off the bottom of the tomato so it can stand upright.

- Slice the flesh downward in a curve as to cut around the seeds.

- After the outer flesh is removed, use your fingers to remove any remaining seeds from the interior and discard. Cut the stem portion off. Dice the remaining tomato.

Preparing the Jalapeño

- You will need to remove the stem and seeds from the jalapeño before dicing it. To remove the stem, slice the top of the jalapeño off and discard.

- Cut the jalapeño in half lengthwise, exposing the seeds and white veins.

- Use a spoon to scrape the seeds and veins away from the flesh and discard. Do this carefully so that the juices do not spray near your face.

APPETIZERS & SNACKS

CHICKEN & CHEESE FLAUTAS

This delicious finger food is a classic Mexican snack and appetizer

Flautas, which were originally named for their flute shape, have become synonymous with *taquitos* ("little tacos"). Both are a tortilla (corn or flour) rolled up with a meat filling. In most recipes taquitos tend to be made with corn tortillas, while flautas are more often made with flour tortillas. You will find arguments for both cases, but there are no debates over the crunchy texture and delicious flavor of either variety.

Flautas traditionally contain shredded meat and melted cheese, which are a popular combination in many Mexican dishes. They are then fried to a crispy and delicious golden color and served immediately. Because flautas need no utensils for eating, they make a nice appetizer. *Yield: Serves 5*

Ingredients

1 1/2 cups shredded chicken

3/4 cup shredded queso quesadilla (mild mexican white cheese)

1/4 cup diced green chiles

3/4 cup green chile sauce

Pinch of salt

10 flour tortillas

10 toothpicks for securing tortillas

Chicken and Cheese Flautas

- Toss the chicken, cheese, chiles, chile sauce, and salt in a bowl until evenly combined.

- Place a tortilla on a flat surface and add 2 tablespoons chicken mixture in a straight line just off center.

- Roll one edge of the tortilla over the filling and slightly under it. Roll it up the rest of the way and secure with a toothpick in the center.

- Fry flauta on both sides until golden and crispy. Remove the toothpicks; serve immediately.

Flautas with Corn Tortillas: If you use store-bought corn tortillas, you want to steam them to make them pliable enough to roll. To do this, wrap 10 tortillas in a damp cloth towel and microwave 90 seconds. Or place tortillas wrapped in a damp towel in a casserole dish and bake 15 minutes at 300°F. Keep them covered and pull out one at a time to use.

Beef Flautas: Use shredded beef and a red chile sauce instead of chicken and green chile sauce. Add a dash of chile powder.

Vegetarian Flautas: Replace the chicken with corn and more chiles and add a pinch of cumin to bring out a zesty flavor.

Filling the Flauta

- To be able to roll the flauta so that the filling is in the center, the filling has to be placed on the tortilla in the correct area.

- Place the filling in a line, halfway between the center and the edge.

- Make sure to extend the filling all the way to the edges of the tortilla.

- It may not seem like enough, but about 2 tablespoons of filling should be sufficient. Add more if you like.

Rolling the Flautas

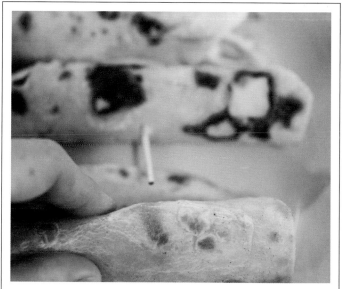

- After you have the filling placed in the correct area, it will be much easier to roll it up.

- Start by taking the side of the tortilla nearest the filling and roll it over the filling. You may need to tuck excess tortilla under the filling.

- Roll the tortilla up the rest of the way, keeping it very tight.

- Insert a toothpick at an angle to keep the flauta rolled.

APPETIZERS & SNACKS

PLANTAIN CHIPS

Crunchy chips made from the starchy plantain are a delicious and healthy snack

Plantains are the starchy cousins of yellow bananas. While yellow bananas are eaten raw, plantains need to be cooked. Because of their firm texture, plantains can be thinly sliced and then fried into chips. A plantain that is ripened to a yellow color is ideal, although green will work too.

In Mexico you will find these salty snacks sold by the bagful.

They are crunchy but have a softer texture than a tortilla chip. They can be enjoyed plain or used to scoop up salsa or guacamole. They are also delicious when tossed in a chile seasoning to give them some heat. They can also be enjoyed without any salt or seasonings to bring out their subtle sweet flavor. *Yield: Serves 3–4*

Plantain Chips

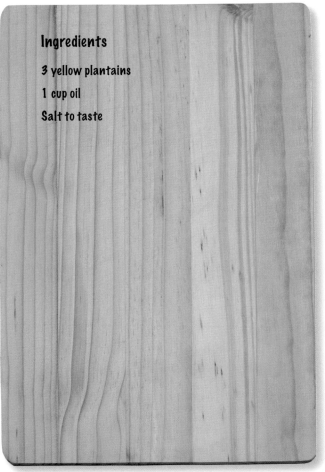

Ingredients

3 yellow plantains

1 cup oil

Salt to taste

- Cut the ends off the plantain and cut the rest into 3 pieces. Score the skin on each piece lengthwise into 6 equal parts. Peel the skin off and discard.

- Slice the plantains with a sharp knife.

- Fry the plantains in oil, turning them often, until each side is slightly golden. They will still be very light in color.

- Remove the chips from the oil and allow to drain on a paper towel to remove some oil. Sprinkle with salt and serve.

Zesty Chile Plantain Chips: For a spicier version, place 2 tablespoons chile powder and 1 teaspoon salt in a large plastic bag. Place enough prepared chips in the bag to fill it about halfway. Seal the bag and gently shake until chile powder evenly covers the chips. Open the bag and serve as usual.

Tangy Lime Plantain Chips: After salting the chips, place them in a large bowl. Squeeze the juice of a lime wedge over the top and gently toss. Repeat 3 or 4 more times and serve.

Preparing the Plantain

- Using a very sharp knife, cut a thin slice crosswise off the plantain. The slices should be about $\frac{1}{16}$ of an inch thick.

- Make sure each slice is uniformly thick from top to bottom or they will cook unevenly.

- Each individual slice needs to be the same thickness.

- There is a tool called a mandoline you can use to create perfectly uniform slices. You can find them at most kitchen supply stores.

Frying the Chips

- Heat the oil in a medium-size pan over medium-hot heat. It is hot enough when a pinch of plantain dropped into the oil quickly sizzles and rises to the top.

- Keep the oil at an even temperature, around 365°F.

- Fry the chips in batches. The chips should have space between them (not overlapping) while they are being fried. They will need to cook 2 to 3 minutes.

- Replace the oil as necessary during the cooking process.

APPETIZERS & SNACKS

TORTILLA CHIPS

Corn tortillas that are fried into crispy, crunchy chips are perfect for dipping

Tortilla chips are made from corn tortillas that have been cut into strips or wedges and then fried until crunchy. The best tortilla chips are thin and crispy and not too greasy. The corn gives them their delicious flavor and sturdy texture.

Tortilla chips were first introduced in the 1940s, and they have since risen in popularity across the world. They are different from corn chips because the corn used to make tortilla chips is treated with lime to soften it for removing the hulls. This changes its taste and texture. A corn chip is corn meal that is pressed and fried. Tortilla chips can be found in your local grocery store and often bought fresh from your local Mexican restaurant. *Yield: Serves 8–10*

Ingredients

12 tortillas

4 cups oil for frying

Salt to taste

Tortilla Chips

- With the tortillas in a stack, slice them in half and then cut each of those stacks in half. Continue until you have 8 stacks of wedges.

- Fry 2 or 3 chips at a time in hot oil until golden and crispy.

- Drain the finished tortilla chips on paper towels. While the chips are still hot, sprinkle with salt.

- Let the chips cool and then serve them with your favorite salsa or dip.

Flour Tortilla Chips: Use flour tortillas instead of corn. Four tortillas don't need quite as long to cook as corn, so remove them from the oil as soon as they are slightly golden brown. Fresh-made flour tortillas work best and make a flaky, crispy chip.

Baked Tortilla Chips: Brush each whole tortilla with a small amount of oil and return to stack. Flip the stack and brush the other side with oil. Cut the stack into wedges. Place the wedges in a single layer on a baking sheet and cook at 350°F 10 minutes.

Frying Tortilla Chips

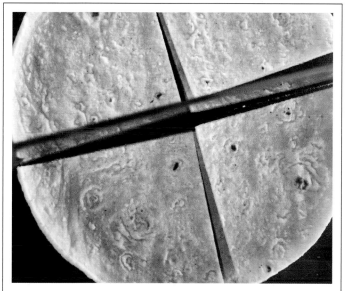

- Heat the oil to 365°F. During the frying process, keep it as close to that temperature as possible.

- The oil is ready when you drop a pinch of tortilla into the oil and it sizzles and rises to the top.

- A deep pan or pot works well for frying tortilla chips. Make sure the oil is at least 2 or 3 inches deep.

- Do not fry the tortilla chips in oil that is not hot enough, or they will absorb too much oil and taste greasy.

Drying Chips on Towel and Serving

- Tortilla chips are superb when served fresh and still warm, although they will still be delicious when cooled.

- The flavor and texture of the tortilla chips pair well with tomato-based salsas.

- The creamy taste of guacamole is another delicious topping and brings out the corn flavor of the chips.

- Since tortilla chips are very sturdy, a thick and hearty bean dip is another great match.

APPETIZERS & SNACKS

PICKLED CARROTS
This tangy and delicious appetizer is quick and easy to prepare

You may have tried these pickled carrots served as an appetizer and condiment in a Mexican restaurant. The tangy pickled flavor is perfectly paired with the slight sweetness of the carrot.

While standard pickling is used to preserve the pickled item, this type of pickled recipe refers more to the tangy flavor than the actual pickling process.

Pickled carrots are enjoyed all over Mexico and the United States as a quick and healthy snack. They can be served alone or alongside a main dish as a condiment.

They are easy to make and will keep will in the refrigerator for up to a week. Pickled carrots are best when eaten the day after preparing them so the flavors have time to absorb into the carrots. *Yield: 6 cups*

Pickled Carrots

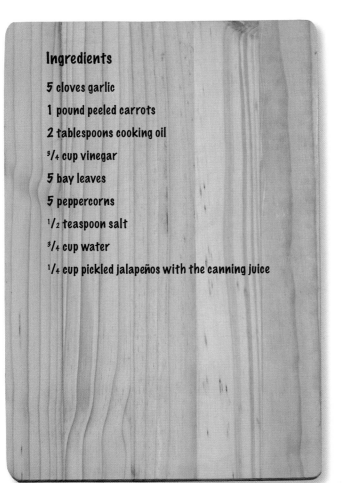

Ingredients

5 cloves garlic

1 pound peeled carrots

2 tablespoons cooking oil

¾ cup vinegar

5 bay leaves

5 peppercorns

½ teaspoon salt

¾ cup water

¼ cup pickled jalapeños with the canning juice

- Peel and chop the garlic cloves. Peel and cut the carrots on the diagonal about ¼-inch thick.

- Heat the oil in a large pan and sauté the garlic and carrots 2 to 3 minutes.

- Slowly add the vinegar, bay leaves, peppercorns, and salt and bring to a simmer 5 minutes.

- Add the water and jalapeños and simmer an additional 10 minutes. Cool the mixture and store in the refrigerator overnight for maximum flavor.

• • • • RECIPE VARIATION • • • •

Pickled Onions: Substitute 1 pound onions for the carrots. Slice and sauté them 1 to 2 minutes. Follow the remaining instructions, but cut the simmering time to 5 minutes total. If the onions begin to soften while being stored, drain the liquid off. You want them to remain somewhat crisp, not soft. Pickled onions can be used as a topping for chicken and fish.

MAKE IT EASY

Before beginning this recipe, assemble all of your supplies and prepare the garlic and carrots. Measure out all the liquids and have them ready to add. If you measure as you go, there is more room for error. Getting everything ready first cuts down on the overall time it takes to prepare a recipe.

Cooking the Carrots

- When you sauté the carrots, be sure to move them around frequently so they cook evenly.

- If you don't have peppercorns, substitute ½ teaspoon ground black or white pepper.

- Make sure to count the bay leaves as you remove them. They do not soften and remain stiff, so they can be a choking hazard.

- You can also tie up the bay leaves and peppercorns in cheesecloth and add it to the pot.

Storing and Serving

- Store the carrots in an airtight container in the refrigerator for up to a week. A bowl-type container works well.

- When you are ready to serve the pickled carrots, use a slotted spoon to remove a serving of carrots, leaving the liquid behind.

- You can add more jalapeños at any point to increase the heat level.

- Pickled carrots are usually served as a small appetizer but can also be enjoyed as part of a main dish.

APPETIZERS & SNACKS

MENUDO

This classic Mexican soup is claimed to have healing properties

This richly flavored soup is very popular throughout Mexico. It is served on holidays and special occasions. Menudo is enjoyed as a main dish or consumed in the early hours of the morning because it is said to help combat a hangover.

Menudo originates from the days when wealthy landowners used up the better cuts of meat and left only the organ meats for the peasants. They had to figure out creative ways to use them and often put them in highly seasoned soups.

Because of the combination of unique ingredients, menudo has a one-of-a-kind flavor. Tripe is the main component of this soup, and it wouldn't be menudo without it. *Yield: Serves 6*

Ingredients

1 tablespoon oil

5 cloves garlic

1 medium onion

3 pounds honeycomb tripe

4 quarts water

1 tablespoon oregano

5 peppercorns

1 4-ounce can diced green chiles

2 cups red chile sauce

1 cup canned hominy

Menudo

- Heat oil in large pot over medium heat. Peel and chop the garlic and onion and sauté until garlic begins to turn golden.

- Rinse the tripe well and cut it into bite-size pieces; add it to the pot.

- Add the water, oregano, peppercorns, chiles, and chile sauce. Bring to a slow simmer.

- Let the soup simmer 3 hours. Add the hominy and cook an additional 30 minutes.

• • • • RECIPE VARIATION • • • •

Calf's Foot or Pig's Feet: Many menudo recipes call for either 1 calf's foot or 2 pig's feet. If you would like to incorporate either one, add it along with the tripe. After the soup cooks, you can either remove the calf's foot or pig's feet to remove the bones and return the meat to the soup, or you can leave them whole.

• • • • • • • • GREEN ● LIGHT • • • • • • • • • • •

Just as important as the soup are the various toppings used to customize each bowl. Chopped cilantro leaves, lemon wedges, or green onions add a fresh flavor. Chopped fresh red chiles or hot chile sauce add tangy flavor and more intense heat. Warm corn or flour tortillas can be dipped into the soup to soak up the last few bites from the bottom of the bowl.

Preparing the Tripe

- Rinse the tripe under running water until the water runs clear. Rub your fingers over it to check for residual grittiness and to see that it's adequately clean; pat dry.

- Tripe is shaped irregularly, so when you get ready to cut it, press it out as flat as you can.

- Cut the tripe lengthwise in strips. Use a sharp knife, as tripe has a bit of a gummy, rubbery texture.

- Take the strips and cut them crosswise to create 1-inch pieces.

Cooking the Menudo

- As the soup simmers, it may be necessary to add more water to replace any that has cooked off. Add boiling hot water 1 cup at a time so it doesn't slow down the cooking process.

- Canned hominy has a soft texture, but you don't want it too mushy. Check the hominy every 5 to 10 minutes during cooking to make sure it is not becoming overcooked.

- If the hominy begins to get too soft, remove the soup from heat and allow it to cool.

SOUPS

POSOLE

Traditional hominy and hearty chunks of pork make this a flavorful soup

This delicious soup is a traditional dish in Mexico, and you will find it in almost every Mexican restaurant. Although the broth is light and flavorful, the hearty chunks of pork make this soup suitable and satisfying enough for a meal.

Posole is thought to be a very comforting soup and is quite popular in the Mexican states of Jalisco and Guerrero, where pozolerías or "Posole Shops" are common. Posole is well-known for hominy, which is a traditional Mexican ingredient that dates back thousands of years. It is made from a special type of corn that is soaked in lime (a canning agent, not the fruit) to remove the hulls. The germ is removed, allowing the hominy to "flower" when cooked. *Yield: Serves 8*

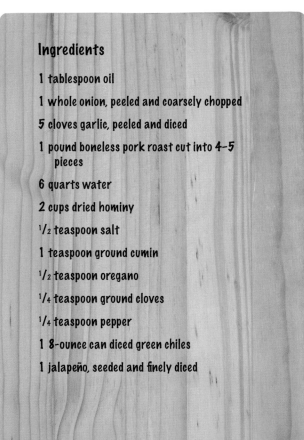

Ingredients

1 tablespoon oil

1 whole onion, peeled and coarsely chopped

5 cloves garlic, peeled and diced

1 pound boneless pork roast cut into 4–5 pieces

6 quarts water

2 cups dried hominy

1/2 teaspoon salt

1 teaspoon ground cumin

1/2 teaspoon oregano

1/4 teaspoon ground cloves

1/4 teaspoon pepper

1 8-ounce can diced green chiles

1 jalapeño, seeded and finely diced

Posole

- Heat the oil in a large pot over medium heat. Add onion, garlic, and pork. Sauté until garlic becomes golden and pork begins to brown.

- Add the water to the pot along with the dried hominy, salt, cumin, oregano, cloves, pepper, chiles, and jalapeños. Simmer 2 hours.

- Remove pork from the liquid and cut into bite-size pieces; return meat to the soup.

- Cook an additional 30 to 45 minutes, until hominy is tender.

Fresh Green Chiles: If you want to use fresh green chiles in place of canned, there are a few extra steps. First char the green chiles on a comal or in the broiler until the skin is black and blistered. Peel off the skin, split the chile open, and scrape out the seeds and veins. The chile can then be chopped and added to the soup.

Frozen Hominy: If you can't find dried hominy, substitute frozen hominy (thaw it out first) or canned hominy. Be sure to add it during the last 30 minutes of cooking so it doesn't get too soft. You can reduce the overall cooking time by 30 minutes as well.

Sautéing the Pork

- Browning the meat is an important flavor component of posole.

- Make sure the heat is high enough to quickly sear the outside but not actually cook the meat.

- Leave the meat in one place, directly touching the hot pan, about 1 minute to brown it. Turn it over and brown each side.

- While the meat is browning, keep the onions and garlic moving so they don't burn.

Serving Posole

- Like most Mexican soups, posole is often served with a selection of toppings.

- Chopped cilantro, chopped fresh Mexican oregano, and lime wedges are wonderful subtle additions that bring out the flavors of the soup.

- For a bolder addition, try chopped fresh onion, sliced radish, or chile sauce to spice up the flavor.

- Soups are always served with a stack of piping hot corn or flour tortillas.

SOUPS

ALBONDIGAS

This is a delicious and simple soup with a light broth and hearty meatballs

Albondigas is a very popular soup, and every family has a cherished recipe. But every family recipe has one thing in common: meatballs. Whether they are made with beef, chorizo, chicken, or turkey, it's not albondigas without them.

This soup originates back to the Spanish conquistadors and their influence over the Mexican diet. They introduced not only new foods but new ways to prepare them, such as grinding meat and forming a meatball.

Albondigas is not hard to make, but the meatballs can be time-consuming, so make sure you have time before you start the recipe. It will take about 20 minutes to make the meatballs. *Yield: Serves 4–6*

Ingredients

1 pound ground beef (or a combination of ¹/₂ pound beef and ¹/₂ pound chorizo)

¹/₂ cup cooked rice

1 egg, beaten

¹/₂ teaspoon salt

2 teaspoons cumin, divided

1 tablespoon oil

3 cloves garlic, peeled and crushed

3 white onions, chopped

3 quarts chicken broth

4 stalks celery, chopped

1 bunch cilantro, leaves only

4 large carrots, peeled and chopped or sliced

2 cups raw spinach

2 teaspoons oregano

Albondigas

- Mix the ground beef, rice, egg, salt, and cumin. Form meatballs about the size of a large marble.

- Heat oil over medium heat and begin to cook the meatballs. Add the garlic and onions and cook until onions begin to wilt.

- Carefully add the remaining ingredients.

- Bring soup to a simmer and let cook 1 hour.

Hint of Mint Albondigas: Some albondigas recipes have a Middle Eastern influence and add fresh mint. Add 4 or 5 chopped mint leaves to the meatball mixture.

Tomato Albondigas: Add 1 cup tomato sauce to the soup during cooking.

Pea and Bean Albondigas: Substitute peas or green beans for the celery.

To save time, make the meatballs a day ahead. Prepare as directed and place in a single layer on a greased 9x13 baking dish. Place a layer of waxed paper over the meatballs and place another layer of meatballs on the wax paper. Continue to layer wax paper and meatballs until all meatballs are made. Cover it with a lid or plastic wrap and keep the meatballs in the fridge up to 24 hours.

Preparing the Meatballs

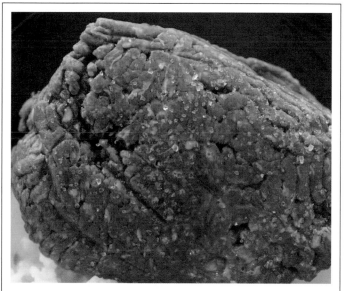

- Great meatballs are important for great albondigas. If you take your time when making them, you will have fantastic results.

- Scoop out 1 heaping teaspoon of meat mixture and place it on your fingertips. Use your fingers and

thumbs to transfer and mold the mixture into a ball.

- After you have formed a meatball, perfect it by rolling it between your palms.

- Treat meatballs with care. If you are too rough, they may fall apart.

Serving Albondigas

- Albondigas doesn't require a lot of garnishes; however it is often served with a spicy chile salsa for those who like a little added heat.

- Green onions and chopped cilantro are sometimes used as garnishes.

- Albondigas is always accompanied by fresh and warm corn or flour tortillas.

- For a heartier soup, albondigas is sometimes served on top of a scoop of cooked white rice.

SOUPS

SOPA DE TORTILLA

Make this classic tortilla soup with beans and rice and top it with tortillas

While there are no specific origins of tortilla soup, the idea of eating soup with tortillas is an ancient concept in Mexico. It's no wonder it evolved into the delicious tortilla soup we enjoy today.

Tortilla soup has become a popular Tex-Mex item with the addition of cheddar cheese and sometimes colorful red and yellow processed corn tortilla strips. But in Mexico, cooks top this soup with Cotija cheese and corn tortilla chips. Cotija is a somewhat hard and salty cheese (similar to parmesan).

If you make the soup ahead of time, be sure to wait to add the tortilla chips or they will become soggy. Add the strips and the cheese just before you serve it. *Yield: Serves 4*

Ingredients

1 tablespoon oil

1 small onion, peeled and chopped

2 cloves garlic, peeled and chopped

2 quarts chicken broth plus 1 cup water

1/2 cup white rice, uncooked

2 large chicken breasts

1 cup cooked or canned black beans

1 cup corn (fresh, frozen, or canned)

1/2 cup chopped cilantro

2 jalapeños, stem and seeds removed.

2 tablespoons ground chile

2 teaspoons ground cumin

1 tablespoon dried oregano

3 corn tortillas cut into 1/4-inch-wide strips

1/3 cup crumbled Cotija or queso fresco

12 slices avocado

1/4 cup oil

Sopa de Tortilla

- In a large pot, heat 1 table-spoon oil over medium-high heat; sauté the onion and garlic. Carefully add the chicken broth and rice; bring to a simmer.

- In a separate pan, cook the chicken breasts, shred them with two forks, and add it to the soup.

- If using canned beans or corn, rinse and drain them.

- Add the beans, corn, cilantro, jalapeños, and seasonings. Simmer 30 minutes and serve topped with a handful of fried tortilla strips, a sprinkle of Cotija, and 12 slices of avocado.

• • • • RECIPE VARIATION • • • •

Sopa de Tortilla with Flour Tortillas: In some versions of Sopa de Tortilla, a flour tortilla is placed in the bowl before the soup. You can do this by pressing a flour tortilla into the bottom of a bowl. Ladle the soup on top of the tortilla; after a few minutes the liquid absorbs into the tortilla, allowing you to use a spoon to scoop up a piece of tortilla with each bite.

MAKE IT EASY

Sopa de Tortilla is pretty simple to make. You can save time by using leftover chicken or cooking and shredding the chicken the day before and refrigerating it for up to 24 hours. You can also use crumbled tortilla chips as the topping if you don't have time to fry your own strips.

Preparing Tortilla Strips

Garnishing Sopa de Tortilla

- Heat ¼ cup oil over medium heat in a medium pan until hot, about 360°F.

- The oil is ready when a small piece of tortilla dropped into the oil sizzles and rises to the top.

- Use a large spoon to scoop up tortilla strips and place them in the pan. Use the spoon to move them around to ensure they fry evenly.

- Remove strips with a slotted spoon when they are golden and crunchy. Drain on paper towels before serving.

- Sprinkle the tortilla strips onto the top of the soup in a pile in the center. This will keep some of the tortillas out of the liquid so they do not get soggy.

- Sprinkle a generous tablespoon of cheese over the top of the tortilla strips and the soup.

- Cotija is an excellent choice because it has a strong flavor and firm texture. Another good choice for cheese is queso fresco.

- Fresh Cotija and queso fresco easily crumble with your fingers.

SOUPS

SOPA DE LIMA

A savory and refreshing soup perfect for a light lunch on a warm day

Lime is a popular flavoring in Mexico and is the key ingredient in this recipe. It livens up what might be a bland chicken soup into a hearty, yet refreshing meal. Limes are easily found in your local grocery store and add amazing zest to this delicious soup.

Another great thing about this soup is that the amount of lime is easily adjusted to suit your taste. You add the lime juice last, and you can taste it as you add it so you get the perfect amount every time.

You will also find tomatillos in this soup, and the lime enhances their tart flavor. Jalapeños add a nice hint of heat, and the onions and garlic round out the dish. *Yield: Serves 4–6*

Ingredients

2 tablespoons cooking oil

$1/2$ medium onion, peeled and chopped

2 cloves garlic, peeled and chopped

4 quarts chicken broth or stock

2 large chicken breasts, freshly broiled or grilled

1 jalapeño, seeds and stem removed

2 tomatillos, husks removed and chopped

2 tablespoons dried oregano

Salt and pepper to taste

1 lime cut into quarters

1 lime cut into slices

Chopped cilantro for garnishing

Sopa de Lima

- In a large pot heat the oil over medium heat and sauté the onion and garlic.

- Carefully pour in the chicken broth and bring to a simmer while you shred the chicken breasts.

- Chop the jalapeño and add to the soup along with the tomatillos, oregano, salt, and pepper.

- Simmer 45 minutes. Squeeze the juice from 1 lime quarter into the soup just before serving. Garnish each bowl with lime slices and cilantro.

• • • • RECIPE VARIATION • • • •

Sopa de Lima with Extra Lime: If you like a more in-depth lime flavor, you can marinate your chicken in ¼ cup of lime juice and a ½ teaspoon of salt for 15 minutes before grilling or broiling. Don't leave the chicken in the lime juice for too long because it will begin to "cook" in the acid. For an intense lime flavor add a few pinches of freshly grated lime zest while the soup is simmering.

MAKE IT EASY

Fresh and juicy limes are imperative for a delicious sopa de lima. Choose limes that are large and bright green with thin skins. Avoid limes that have unripened yellow areas or soft spots. When you cut them open, the flesh should appear juicy and not dry, and if you cannot locate fresh, juicy limes, substitute a jar of store-bought lime juice.

Shredding the Chicken

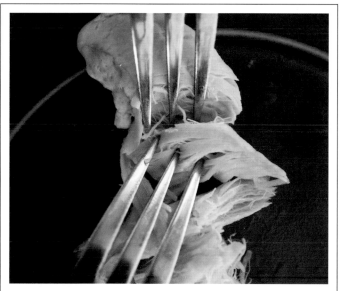

- If the chicken is cool enough, use your fingers to pull it apart into bite-size chunks.

- If the chicken is too hot to touch, shred it with two forks.

- With one fork in each hand, place the prongs downward into the chicken back-to-back, then pull the forks apart to shred the chicken.

- Work on a cutting board or stable work surface, as a plate may slide around and be difficult to manage.

Serving Sopa de Lima

- Sopa de Lima is often served with lime slices floating on the top and a sprinkle of chopped cilantro.

- The lime slices should be very thin. Use a sharp knife and slice uniform pieces about ⅛ inch or less.

- Alternatively, you can serve lime wedges on the side to be squeezed into the soup as desired.

- Serve Sopa de Lima with hot, fresh flour tortillas.

SOUPS

CARNE EN SU JUGO

This satisfying beef soup is flavored with smoky bacon and onions

Carne en su jugo (beef soup with bacon and beans) is a classic Mexican comfort food. The smokiness of the bacon adds delicious warmth, and the hearty chunks of beef are tender and flavorful. It is a popular soup in the Mexican city of Guadalajara, where there is a restaurant that holds the Guinness World Record for the fastest service because their only menu item is carne en su jugo.

While there are quite a few variations of this soup, there are two ingredients that are always used: beef and bacon. The bacon is what gives the soup its signature flavor; you can't call it carne en su jugo without it. *Yield: Serves 6*

Ingredients

¹/₂ **pound lean bacon, chopped**

2 **pounds top round beef steak, chopped into small, bite-size pieces**

1 **medium onion, peeled and chopped**

4 **quarts beef broth or stock**

¹/₂ **cup cilantro leaves, chopped**

2 **cups black beans, homemade or canned**

Carne en su Jugo

- Heat a large pot over medium heat and brown the bacon pieces. When they are almost finished cooking, add the beef and onion.

- Keeping the ingredients moving, cook 2 to 3 more minutes or until bacon is browned and crispy.

- Add the beef broth or stock and cilantro to the pot. Rinse and drain the beans and add them to the soup.

- Simmer 1 hour and serve hot with a variety of garnishes.

Carne en su Jugo with Tomatillos: To add a touch of tanginess to your soup, add 3 to 4 chopped tomatillos when you add the beans.

Carne en su Jugo with Black Beans: While black beans add a delicious earthy flavor, you can certainly use pinto beans in their place.

Spicy Carne en su Jugo: For more flavor and heat, add a 4-ounce can of diced jalapeños. Drain the juice from the can before adding to the soup.

Garnishes for Carne en su Jugo: Make a stack of un-cooked tortillas while the soup is simmering. Then cook a couple of tortillas for each person as you serve the soup. For the ultimate experience, make a batch of fresh salsa the day before and serve as a garnish.

Selecting the Beef

Serving Carne en su Jugo

- Carne en su Jugo is only as good as the quality of beef used. Make sure you use the freshest beef possible.

- You can find fresh-cut beef at your local butcher or *car-niceria*, which is a Mexican meat market.

- Look for bright red color and virtually no marbling, as top round is not a very fatty cut of meat.

- If top round in unavailable, substitute flank or round steak.

- For the best flavor, serve Carne en su Jugo immedi-ately. It does not benefit from extended cooking.

- Keep it warm while it is being served in case any-one wants more, as reheat-ing it changes the flavor.

- Carne en su Jugo is a simple dish not requiring a lot of garnishes, but salsa is a popular addition you can provide.

- Make sure to have a supply of fresh and warm flour or corn tortillas to enjoy with the soup.

SOUPS

ENCHILADAS VERDE

Featuring green chile sauce and chicken, this classic Mexican dish is a crowd-pleaser

Enchiladas have a long and varied history in Mexican cuisine. There are hundreds, if not thousands, of varieties with unique and flavorful fillings and sauces. Enchilada means "in chile," and the earliest enchiladas were simply a tortilla dipped in chile sauce and then rolled up and eaten. They have since evolved to include meats, cheeses, vegetables, and more.

Enchiladas verde gets its name from the green chile sauce used to flavor the dish. Chicken is a common filling for enchiladas verde as is fresh Mexican cheese. *Yield: Serves 4–6*

Ingredients

12 corn tortillas

$\frac{1}{2}$ cup cooking oil

2 cups shredded chicken

1 29-ounce can green chile sauce

1 $\frac{1}{2}$ cups shredded or crumbled queso fresco or queso blanco

1 4-ounce can diced green chiles

$\frac{1}{4}$ cup crumbled Cotija cheese

Enchiladas Verde

- Lightly brush tortillas with cooking oil. Heat one on a comal over medium heat.

- Remove warm tortilla and place chicken, a drizzle of chile sauce, and cheese down the center.

- Roll tortilla around filling; place seam side down in 9x13 inch baking dish. Repeat with remaining tortillas, chicken, sauce, and cheese.

- Pour remaining chile sauce over the top. Sprinkle with diced green chiles and any remaining cheese. Bake at 350°F 35 minutes. Top with Cotija before serving.

• • • • RECIPE VARIATIONS • • • •

Enchiladas Suiza: Add some fresh chopped spinach to the filling and drizzle a white cream sauce over the top of the rolled tortillas before baking. To make a quick and easy cream sauce, whisk together $1/2$ cup Crema Agria (sour cream), a 5-ounce can evaporated milk, and 4 ounces crumbled Cotija.

Shredded Pork Enchiladas: Simmer a pork roast in water with a can of jalapeños or chipotle chiles in adobo sauce. After the pork is tender, remove it from the liquid and pull it apart into bite-size chunks. Use the shredded pork instead of the chicken for delicious results.

Preparing the Tortillas

- Use good-quality cooking oil for the tortillas. Vegetable or peanut oil are nice choices and will add flavor.

- Lightly coat each side of each tortilla with the oil and place the tortillas in a stack on a plate.

- Heat a comal over medium-high heat and cook each tortilla about 15 seconds on each side.

- The idea is not to cook them or get them crispy, you just want to soften them with the heat.

Rolling the Tortillas

- Rolling the tortillas around the filling is actually more of a folding technique.

- Fold one side of the tortilla over the filling and hold it down while you overlap the other edge to create a seam.

- Turn the rolled tortilla over so the seam is on the bottom of the dish. The weight of the filling should keep it closed.

- If the edges do not overlap, you have used too much filling. Simply remove some and try again.

CHILE-LIME CHICKEN

Grilled chicken is enhanced with savory seasonings and a tangy kick of lime

This recipe is a simple way to pack a lot of flavor into an otherwise bland cut of chicken. The chiles add an earthy taste and some heat, while the garlic rounds out the flavors. The lime juice in the marinade penetrates into the chicken and keeps it tender while complementing the chile with a bit of tanginess.

Although many people like to boil their chicken before grilling it, to keep the chicken from drying out, Mexicans do not utilize that step and will grill the chicken until it is charred but moist and juicy on the inside.

This Chile-Lime Chicken is the perfect addition to any barbecue or potluck. When it's cooking on the grill, the aroma filling the air will have your mouth watering. *Yield: Serves 5*

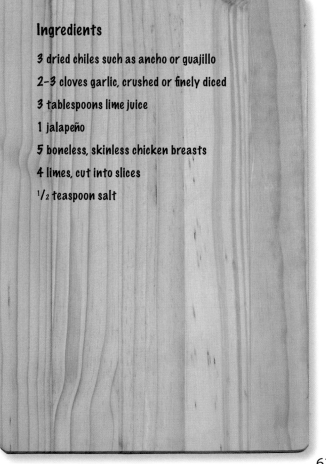

Ingredients

3 dried chiles such as ancho or guajillo

2–3 cloves garlic, crushed or finely diced

3 tablespoons lime juice

1 jalapeño

5 boneless, skinless chicken breasts

4 limes, cut into slices

¹/₂ teaspoon salt

Chile-Lime Chicken

- Remove stems and seeds from the chiles and soak in warm water 30 minutes, until softened.

- For the marinade, puree the chiles with the garlic, lime juice, and jalapeño. Add a little chile soaking liquid if it is too thick.

- Place chicken, lime slices and salt in a glass baking dish; add the marinade. Pierce each chicken breast with a fork.

- Cover and refrigerate 30 minutes. Remove chicken from marinade and cook on a medium-hot grill until cooked through.

•••• RECIPE VARIATIONS ••••

Chile–Lime-Orange Chicken: If you don't have fresh limes, or you just want another option, use 2 tablespoons orange juice and 1 tablespoon lime juice. The chile and orange combination is very typical in the Yucatan region of Mexico. You can substitute a canned or pickled jalapeño for the fresh one. If you have jalapeño rings, use 6 in place of 1 whole jalapeño.

Dark Meat Chile-Lime Chicken: Use chicken thighs in place of the breasts. They have a slightly stronger flavor than breasts, but the chile flavors will go well with the dark meat. Since dark meat is naturally juicier than breast, you can forgo piercing it with a fork.

Tenderizing the Chicken

- Tenderize the chicken with a fork to allow the marinade to fully penetrate the chicken.

- Place the chicken into a large glass baking dish in a single layer and coat with the marinade.

- Pierce each piece of chicken about 15 to 20 times.

- Turn each piece over and repeat on the other side. Cover the chicken with a lid or plastic wrap and refrigerate.

Grilling the Chicken

- Heat the grill to medium heat.

- Use tongs or a fork to pick up each piece of chicken and let some of the marinade drip off for a moment; then place it onto the grill.

- Turn the chicken every 3 minutes to ensure even

cooking. Check the chicken after 15 minutes for doneness.

- The chicken is done when the interior reaches 170°F and the juices run clear. Let the chicken rest 1 minute to let the juices distribute evenly.

CHICKEN IN PEANUT SAUCE

A moist and tender chicken breast smothered in a creamy peanut sauce

This dish is known as pollo encacahuatado. In the hot and humid state of Veracruz on the Gulf of Mexico, nuts and seeds are often used to add creaminess and flavor to sauces. Pollo Encacahuatado is no exception with its creamy peanut-based sauce.

Peanuts were first used by the Mayans and eventually made their way through the Americas. They are used in the Veracruz area more than anywhere else in Mexico.

The use of peanuts and chiles in this recipe represents the culture and flavor of Veracruzan cuisine. The ingredients for the sauce are easily found, and the sauce is delicious over any cut of chicken, light or dark. *Yield: Serves 6*

Ingredients

¹⁄₄ cup peanut oil plus 2 tablespoons, divided

6 boneless, skinless chicken breasts

1¹⁄₂ cups water

3 plum tomatoes, diced

¹⁄₂ onion, diced

1 dried red chile, seeds and stem removed

³⁄₄ cup unsalted peanuts

2–3 cloves garlic, peeled

1³⁄₄ cups chicken broth

Salt to taste

Chicken in Peanut Sauce

- In a large saucepan, heat ¼ cup oil over high heat; brown the chicken on each side.

- Add the water and simmer the chicken until it is cooked to 170°F. While the chicken is cooking, make the sauce.

- In a separate pot heat 2 tablespoons oil; add remaining ingredients and simmer 15 minutes.

• • • • RECIPE VARIATION • • • •

Easy Substitutions: If you don't have fresh peanuts, substitute ½ cup unsweetened peanut butter. The peanut oil called for in the recipe adds a light nutty flavor, but you can use cooking oil if necessary. You can also use skinless, boneless chicken thighs instead of breasts or serve the sauce over pieces of a whole roasted chicken.

ZOOM

Because the sauce is rich and creamy, a lighter side dish, such as steamed vegetables, grilled squash, or a fresh side salad would be a good match. Beans and rice would be a more authentic choice for a side dish, but might make for a heavier meal.

Simmering the Chicken

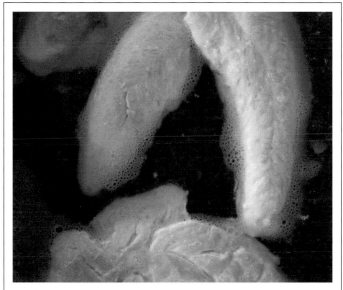

- After you have browned the chicken in the hot oil to sear the juices in and add texture, simmer it to keep it moist.

- Add the water to the pan with the browned chicken.

- Cover and let it simmer about 10 minutes, then remove the lid and continue to simmer.

- After water has cooked off, the chicken should be ready. The internal temperature should be 170°F.

Blending the Sauce

- You have a couple of options to blend the sauce; both deliver similar results.

- The easiest way is to use a stick blender to blend the sauce right in the pan.

- Another option is to let the ingredients cool and then blend the sauce in a blender; return sauce to the pan and reheat.

- Never place hot liquids into a blender. It could cause the lid to come off and spray the contents everywhere.

POLLO FUNDIDO

This dish combines the delicious flavors of juicy chicken with melted cheese

This delicious chicken dish is a more recent addition to Mexican cooking. While the exact origins of the creation of the first pollo fundido are not known, it is now a common menu item in many Mexican restaurants.

Most pollo fundido recipes include cream cheese, which is not a widely used ingredient in Mexican cooking, although it is gaining popularity. The cream cheese adds a unique flavor and creamy texture to the sauce, and the cumin and ground chile give the filling its classic Mexican flavors. The fried outer shell adds texture to this well-rounded dish.

Pollo Fundido is easy to prepare and makes a delicious meal any time of day. *Yield: Serves 5*

Ingredients

1 tablespoon oil

6 boneless, skinless chicken breasts

3 cloves garlic, crushed

$1/2$ cup chopped onion

1 bell pepper, chopped

1 stalk celery, chopped

$1/4$ teaspoon ground cumin

$1/2$ teaspoon ground chile powder

$1/2$ teaspoon salt

$1/4$ cup red chile sauce

10 medium flour tortillas

2 cups cooking oil

Fundido sauce

1 cup grated queso Chihuahua or Manchego
    cheese

Pollo Fundido

- Heat the oil in a large saucepan over medium heat. Cut the chicken into bite-size pieces and cook 5 minutes.

- Add the garlic, onion, vegetables, seasonings, and chile sauce; cook until the chicken is done and the vegetables have softened.

- Roll the chicken filling into the tortillas and fry in hot oil until golden on each side.

- Top with Fundido Sauce and grated cheese. Broil until the cheese is melted.

• • • • RECIPE VARIATIONS • • • •

Fundido Sauce: Place 4 ounces cream cheese; $^1/_2$ cup Crema Agria; $^1/_2$ cup heavy cream; 1 garlic clove, crushed;,and 1 jalapeño, seeds and stem removed, into a blender. Pulse on low speed until well combined.

Make It an Appetizer: Queso Fundido is a delicious and

filling main dish but can easily be made into bite-size appetizers. Use twenty-five small, taco-size (sometimes referred to as fajita-size) flour tortillas instead of the larger ones. Use 2 tablespoons of filling and prepare them as directed in the recipe. Skip the broiling, and serve the Fundido sauce as a dip on the side.

Frying the Stuffed Tortilla

- Place an equal amount of filling vertically down the center of each tortilla.

- Fold the top edge of the tortilla about 2 inches over the top of the filling; repeat with the bottom edge.

- Wrap the side of the tortilla over the filling and wrap the other side over that. If necessary, use a toothpick to secure it.

- Heat 2 cups oil over medium-high heat and cook the tortilla on each side until golden brown.

Adding the Creamy Cheese Sauce

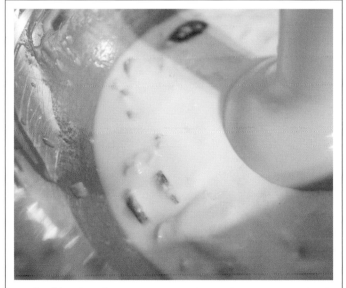

- After blending the sauce, keep it in the refrigerator until you are ready to serve Pollo Fundido.

- When it's time to serve, drizzle an equal amount of the cheese sauce over each filled tortilla.

- Top with a generous pile of shredded cheese. You can substitute Monterey Jack cheese if necessary.

- Place the Pollo Fundido under the broiler until the cheese is melted and starts to brown. Serve immediately.

SALSA CHICKEN

This slow-cooked chicken dish is a perfect filling for tacos, burritos, or enchiladas

This recipe is very easy to make and calls for only 4 ingredients. The long cooking time makes the chicken incredibly juicy and tender. The salsa helps to marinate the chicken and create a delicious sauce with classic Mexican flavor.

You can place some Salsa Chicken in a steamed corn tortilla and top it with onions and cilantro for a delicious meal. Or try it in a burrito with rice and beans. Chicken was introduced to Mexico by the Spanish conquistadores, and tomatoes were native ingredients, so it was probably easy to start mixing the new ingredients with the old to create delicious new flavors. While this recipe is a modern take on those flavors, they represent authentic Mexican cooking. *Yield: Serves 6*

Ingredients

6 boneless, skinless chicken breasts

2 tablespoons oil

3 cups chicken broth

1 1/2 cups fresh salsa

Salsa Chicken

- In a hot pan, brown the chicken in the oil about 1 minute per side.

- In a separate large pot, bring chicken broth to a simmer. Add the chicken and salsa; bring to a simmer.

- Simmer 2 hours or until the liquid evaporates, leaving just chicken and salsa. Add water if the liquid evaporates too quickly.

- Shred the chicken and serve immediately.

···· RECIPE VARIATIONS ····

Different Salsas: For intense heat and bright, refreshing flavors, use a habañero salsa. Right before serving, add a few squeezes from a lime wedge. Salsa verde also makes a delicious choice for this dish, with its tangy flavors and beautiful green color. Try experimenting with salsas to find your favorite.

Slow-Cooker Salsa Chicken: Reduce the chicken broth by 1 cup and add it to the slow cooker with the chicken and salsa. Cook on low heat for 8 hours. Shred the chicken as directed.

Browning the Chicken

- Heat the oil in a pan over high heat about 2 minutes or until very hot.

- Carefully add chicken breasts to the pan. The chicken will sizzle and possibly splatter, so be sure you are protected.

- Brown the chicken on each side until it has a nice crispy coating.

- At this time the chicken is still raw inside so be cautious.

Serving Salsa Chicken

- Salsa Chicken is a wonderful filling for many Mexican dishes including tacos, burritos, and enchiladas.

- Try serving this dish buffet style with a stack of warm corn and flour tortillas and a selection of garnishes.

- Garnishes that go well with Salsa Chicken include chopped onion, chopped cilantro, shredded lettuce or cabbage, hot chile sauce, diced green chiles, jalapeño rings, sour cream, and/or guacamole.

POLLO PIBIL

This Yucatan chicken dish gets its flavor from banana leaves

Pollo pibil is a typical dish in the Yucatan region of Mexico. The Yucatan Peninsula is divided from the rest of Mexico by mountains, and before modern transportation, the terrain prevented travel between the mainland and the tropical peninsula. But the area did have seaports, which were exposed to European and Caribbean influences, and many dishes reflect that. The Yucatan has retained its classic ingredients,

and the dishes served today have not changed much from their original versions.

The banana leaves used to steam Pollo Pibil are a great example of the tropical influence, and bitter oranges are also a key ingredient to many Yucatan dishes. *Yield: Serves 6*

Pollo Pibil

Ingredients

2 tablespoons achiote paste

3 cloves garlic, crushed

1/2 teaspoon salt

4 bitter oranges, juiced

6 boneless, skinless chicken breasts

1 large or 2 small banana leaves

4 tomatoes, sliced

1 onion, peeled and sliced

1 sprig epazote, chopped

1/2 cup unsalted butter, melted

- In a glass baking dish, whisk together the achiote paste, garlic, salt, and orange juice.

- Add the chicken, coating it with marinade; marinate 3 hours in the refrigerator.

- Place the chicken on a banana leaf and top with tomatoes, onion, a pinch of epazote, and a drizzle of butter.

- Wrap the leaf around the chicken, secure it with string, and bake over a large bowl of water for 1 hour.

···· RECIPE VARIATIONS ····

Cochinita Pibil: Replace the chicken with boneless chunks of pork roast.

No Bitter Oranges? If you don't have bitter oranges, use the juice of 3 tangerines and a lime or the juice of 3 oranges and a lemon.

Substitutes for Banana Leaves: Banana leaves are what make this dish special and authentic, but if you cannot locate them, steam the chicken in packets of parchment paper or foil. If you use foil, enclose it so that it is nearly airtight and forgo the bowl of water, as the chicken will steam in the foil packet.

Wrapping the Chicken

- Banana leaves are very large and may need to be cut before use. Three feet long should be adequate.

- To wrap the chicken, fold the edges up over the top like a package.

- Secure with a piece of string to keep the edges down, or use two to secure it from both sides like a parcel.

- Banana leaves have pointy edges, so be careful so that you are not pricked by one.

Serving the Pollo Pibil

- Pollo Pibil is usually served with Yucatan-style side dishes indicative of the region.

- Classic side dishes of white rice and black beans would make excellent companions for Pollo Pibil.

- Squash is another ingredient widely used in the Yucatan and would make a great side dish.

- Garnishes such as thinly sliced onions and habañero salsa make perfect additions.

CHILE COLORADO

This hearty red chile and beef stew is flavorful and satisfying any time of day

The key ingredient in this recipe is the flavorful guajillo chile, which is one of the most common chiles grown in Mexico. Guajillos are leathery and deep red, almost brown in color, which gives this dish its signature red hue. The dried chiles are roasted first to create a deep, smoky flavor. Guajillos are fairly hot and add significant heat to Chile Colorado.

To make milder Chile Colorado, substitute all or part of the guajillo chiles for a milder chile. Anaheim or New Mexico chiles are similar in size and are very mild compared to the guajillo. Look for chiles that are uniform in color and texture with no broken skins. *Yield: Serves 6*

Ingredients

3 quarts water

3 pounds beef roast

¼ cup cooking oil for frying

1 15-ounce can beef broth

1 15-ounce can tomato sauce

1 tablespoon dried oregano

1 teaspoon salt

Chile paste

Chile Colorado

- Pour the water into a large pot; add the beef roast and simmer 3 hours or until fork-tender.

- Remove the beef and pull it into bite-size chunks with forks or your fingers.

- Drain the liquid and add the oil to the pot. Briefly fry the chunks of beef and drain on a paper towel.

- Add the beef broth, tomato sauce, oregano, salt, and chile paste to the pot and simmer 30 minutes.

Chile Paste: Cut the stems off of 8 dried guajillo chiles and cut them open to remove the seeds. Soak them in a bowl of warm water for about 30 minutes, or until softened. Place rehydrated chiles, 2 cloves garlic, $1/2$ cup chopped onion, and 1 jalapeño (seeds and stems removed) into a food processor; and blend until ingredients are thoroughly combined. Drizzle in soaking liquid until the mixture has the consistency of a thin paste, up to $1/2$ cup. Discard any remaining soaking liquid.

Preparing the Chiles

- Pick dried chiles that look fresh and have no tears or broken pieces.

- Rinse the chiles and pat them dry. Cut the top off of each chile and then slit it down the middle.

- Because a dried chile has dry, leathery skin, use kitchen scissors to do the job faster.

- Open the chile and shake out the seeds. Use a spoon, if necessary, to scrape out any seeds that are stuck.

Drying Meat and Serving

- Serve Chile Colorado with a stack of warm corn or flour tortillas to absorb the extra sauce at the bottom of the bowl.

- To liven up the flavor of Chile Colorado, provide a small dish of chopped onions and cilantro.

- If you use a mild chile in the recipe, provide some hot chile sauce to kick up the heat level for those that prefer it.

SEASONED GROUND BEEF
Use this seasoned ground beef as a filling for tacos and more

This ground beef seasoning is flavorful and versatile and easily replaces those packets of store-bought taco seasoning.

Beef is not a native Mexican ingredient; the Spanish introduced it in the 1500s. The native Mexicans quickly incorporated beef into their diets. The grinding of meat dates back thousands of years and is used in many Mexican dishes including picadillo. Ground meat is used as a filling for tacos,

burritos, and enchiladas. You can use the seasoning in this recipe for other recipes such as chicken or pork dishes. *Yield: Serves 4*

Ingredients

1 pound ground beef

¹/₄ cup water

2 tablespoons oregano

1 teaspoon cumin

2 teaspoons garlic powder

2 teaspoons onion powder

¹/₂ teaspoon salt

¹/₄ cup red chile sauce

Seasoned Ground Beef

- Heat a large pan over medium heat. Add ground beef and break it up with a spatula.

- Continue breaking up the beef and mix it around so that it browns evenly.

- Add water to the pan and bring it to a simmer.

- Add the seasonings and chile sauce and continue to simmer until the liquid evaporates and a sauce has formed.

Chile and Tomato Substitutions: If you don't have red chile sauce on hand, substitute 2 tablespoons chile powder and increase the water to $1/2$ cup. If you use the chile powder, add $1/4$ cup tomato sauce or even fresh chopped tomatoes instead of the extra water. The tomato sauce will give the dish some moisture.

Make Extra: This seasoning is great to make ahead of time. Just substitute 2 tablespoons chile powder for the chile sauce. You can even make a triple batch and store it in a cool, dry location so that you can use it whenever you need a delicious Mexican flavor. Sprinkle it on chicken, fish, and over salads for a zesty flavor.

Selecting and Browning Beef

- Ground beef comes in many varieties. Some are made from leftover cuts of meat, others are made from specific cuts.

- The leftover cuts are often the extra pieces from some very expensive cuts, mixed in with some lower quality pieces. But overall it is a good choice for flavor and texture.

- Heat your pan over medium heat for about 1 minute before adding the meat. When you add the meat, break it up quickly so that it does not stick to the bottom of the pan.

Simmering the Beef

- Add the liquid carefully to the hot pan, as it will probably sizzle and could sputter out of the pan.

- Keep the liquid at a very slow simmer. You want the seasonings to have plenty of time to cook with the meat.

- If the water cooks off sooner than 5 minutes, add another $1/4$ cup.

- Remove from the heat as soon as there is no watery liquid remaining in the pan.

MACHACA

Marinated and slowly simmered, this beef dish originated in northern Mexico

Before refrigeration, beef was cooked, shredded, seasoned, and dried. The resulting beef was often eaten in its dried state similar to beef jerky. Sometimes the dried beef was re-hydrated and tenderized and used in recipes that called for fresh beef. This rehydrated beef was called machaca.

While this dried beef is still made in small quantities, machaca now refers to beef that is cooked and shredded in its own juices. Sometimes quite a bit of the liquid is left, which makes for a juicier result. The meat can also be cooked until all the liquid has evaporated, resulting in a drier meat; this is more like the original machaca. *Yield: Serves 6-8*

Ingredients

2 tablespoons cooking oil

3 pounds flank or skirt steak

1 medium onion, diced

1/2 bell pepper, diced

4 cloves garlic, crushed

1 jalapeño, seeds and stem removed

5 medium-size tomatoes, chopped

2 cups beef broth

1 tablespoon oregano

1 teaspoon ground cumin

Machaca

- Cut steak into 5 or 6 pieces; place in a glass dish: Pour marinade over the meat and rub it in for one minute. Cover and refrigerate 18 hours.

- Heat oil. Sear meat in a hot frying pan over high heat, a few pieces at a time; remove.

- Add onion, pepper, garlic, jalapeño, and tomatoes to the pan; sauté.

- Slowly and carefully add the broth, meat, and seasonings. Cover and simmer 2 hours.

- Remove lid and simmer until liquid has evaporated. Shred the meat.

• • • • RECIPE VARIATION • • • •

Marinade for Machaca: In a medium bowl whisk together $1/4$ cup red chile sauce; $1/4$ cup Worcestershire sauce; 1 teaspoon maggi sauce (or soy sauce); 2 tablespoons lime juice; 2 cloves garlic, crushed; $1/2$ teaspoon cumin seed; 1 teaspoon oregano; $1/2$ teaspoon salt; and $1/2$ cup vegetable or olive oil until well combined. You can substitute $1/4$ teaspoon ground cumin for the cumin seeds. Use marinade immediately or refrigerate up to 48 hours.

Cooking the Machaca

- Trim any excess fat or sinew from the meat before cooking.

- After the meat has been removed from the pan, immediately add the onion, pepper, garlic, jalapeño, and tomatoes and begin to sauté.

- Use a spatula to scrape the brown bits off the bottom of the pan left from browning the meat.

- Sauté the vegetables and chiles for three to five minutes or until they begin to soften.

Simmering & Shredding the Meat

- Even though this recipe is not for dried meat, machaca is typically dried in long, thin shreds.

- For an authentic appearance, let it cool slightly and pull the meat from the edges in long pieces.

- You can use two forks to shred the meat if it is too hot to touch and you do not have time to let it cool.

- You can also use a knife to cut it into chunks if it is too hot to touch.

CARNE ASADA

Carne asada is one of the most well-known authentic Mexican dishes north of the border

Carne Asada is a grilled or barbecued meat dish that can be eaten as a steak with side dishes or cut into bite-size pieces and used as a filling for tacos or burritos. It is also the type of meat that is sliced and used for the Tex-Mex dish called fajitas.

You can buy carne asada preperada, meaning the meat is already marinated and ready to be cooked, but making your own marinade allows you to customize the flavors and use the freshest ingredients.

The cut of meat used for Carne Asada is called "skirt steak" and is long and flat. It comes from the belly portion of the cow and is considered to be a tough cut of meat but also very flavorful. *Yield: Serves 4–6*

Ingredients

5–6 dried red chiles such as guajillo, cascabel, or New Mexico

3 tablespoons fresh-squeezed lime juice

$1/4$ teaspoon cumin

2–3 pounds skirt steak

Carne Asada

- Rehydrate and puree the dried chiles with the lime juice, cumin, and ¼ cup of the soaking liquid.

- Prepare the steak, removing any excess membranes and fat. Place in a glass dish.

- Prepare the marinade. Pour the marinade over the steak and marinate in the refrigerator a minimum of 1 hour and up to 24 hours.

- On a hot grill, sear the meat 2 minutes each side; reduce heat to medium and slowly cook until steak is medium well.

• • • • RECIPE VARIATION • • • •

Flank Steak or Flap Meat: If skirt steak is unavailable, you can substitute a thin flank steak. While the texture is a bit chewier, it also is very flavorful. Flap meat is another cut that can be used and is from an area between the flank steak and the bottom sirloin and is very similar in texture to skirt steak, but not quite as flavorful.

ZOOM

The type of chile used for the Carne Asada marinade can make a huge difference in the flavor and heat of Carne Asada. If you want a very mild and earthy flavor, New Mexico, California, or Ancho chiles are great choices. For a spicier marinade, try pasilla chiles or add a pequin chile with the milder ones to spice it up.

Preparing the Steak

- Because skirt steak is from the tough, belly area of the cow, it often has a thin membrane that needs to be removed before cooking.

- Slide a sharp paring knife between the membrane and the meat. Use a slight sawing motion and pull the membrane up while care-fully sliding the knife under it.

- After removing the membranes and any gristle, rinse the meat in cold water to remove excess bone fragments or membranes; pat dry.

Preparing the Marinade

- Prepare the dried chiles by cutting off the stems. Cut the chile in half and shake the seeds out. Pull out any additional white veins that remain.

- Place the chiles in a bowl of hot water and soak 30 minutes.

- Place the chiles in a food processor with about ¼ cup of the soaking liquid and the lime juice, cumin, and salt.

- Process until all the ingredients are well combined.

MILANESAS

A delicious thin slice of beef that has been breaded and fried until crispy

Milanesa is a common dish in South America and is gaining popularity in Mexico. Although it is quite popular in some areas, it is still unknown in some regions of Mexico.

A milanesa is a thin slice of beef, or a cut of beef that has been pounded thin, that is dipped into an egg mixture and then breaded with seasoned bread crumbs or flour. It is then panfried on each side until beef is cooked through and the breading is brown and crispy. They are often served as a *torta* (sandwich) with usual sandwich toppings, but can also be enjoyed as a main course as well. *Yield: Serves 4–6*

Ingredients

3 eggs, beaten

2 cloves garlic, crushed

1 teaspoon chile powder

$^1/_2$ teaspoon salt

$^1/_2$ teaspoon black pepper

1 cup flour

2 pounds beef steaks, sliced very thin ($^1/_8$-inch thick)

$^1/_2$ cup oil for frying

4 bolillo rolls, cut in half and lightly toasted

1 cup shredded lettuce

1 avocado, cut into slices

$^1/_2$ cup red chile sauce

Milanesas

- Whisk together the eggs and garlic. Let it sit 2 minutes to allow the garlic to flavor the egg.

- In another bowl, mix the chile powder, salt, and pepper into the flour. Dip each piece of beef into the egg, then into the flour mixture.

- Fry beef on both sides in hot oil until cooked through and breading is golden.

- Serve on a bolillo roll topped with lettuce, avocado slices, and red chile sauce.

Veal or Chicken Milanesas: In Mexico *milanesa* refers to the preparation method of breading and frying a thin piece of meat rather than specifically to the type of meat. Although beef is the most common milanesa, you can make chicken or veal milanesas by pounding it thin and following the recipe. If you use chicken, boneless, skinless chicken breast works well because it can be cooked quickly.

Serving Suggestions: Milanesas make a great buffet-style meal. Serve up hot and fresh bolillo rolls along with plates of sandwich garnishes such as shredded lettuce, tomato slices, avocado slices, cheese slices, chopped green olives, and hot chile sauce. You can also provide condiments such as mayonnaise and salsa. Provide a plate of freshly fried milanesas, and everyone can build their own sandwich.

Breading the Meat

- When you mix the garlic into the egg, it may appear clumpy. That is okay, as the garlic will flavor the egg as it rests.

- You may need to whisk the egg mixture again after it rests.

- Make sure the salt, pepper, and seasonings are well mixed into the flour.

- Quickly dredge the egg-dipped beef in the flour on each side and make sure it gets coated evenly.

Frying the Meat

- Heat the oil over medium heat. It is ready when a drop of egg sizzles and rises to the top.

- Make sure the oil is not too hot or the breading will burn before the meat has a chance to cook.

- Fry two pieces of meat at a time and drain on paper towels to remove excess oil.

- Do not overcrowd the pan or the oil will drop in temperature, resulting in soggy and greasy Milanesas.

PICADILLO

This classic Latin American dish features ground beef, onions, and tomatoes

Picadillo is one of those dishes that you can adjust for what you have on hand. It is very flexible and tastes great with just about any addition or substitution. The ingredients also vary from region to region. Picadillo in northern Mexico is made with chiles and tomatoes, and in the Yucatan region it is often cooked with peas, carrots, and green olives. It can be a simple dish with only five or six ingredients, or it can be more complex with twenty or more ingredients.

The exact origins of picadillo are unknown, but it has been prepared in Mexico since the 1800s. It is also popular in Puerto Rico and Cuba, where it is often used to stuff pastelitos, which are small meat pies. *Yield: Serves 6*

Picadillo

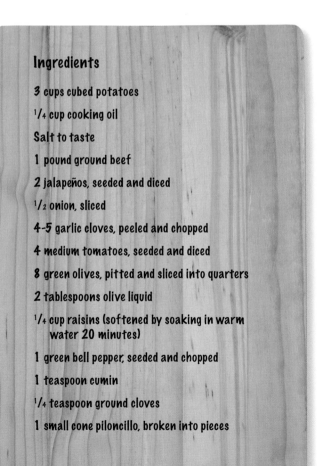

Ingredients

3 cups cubed potatoes

1/4 cup cooking oil

Salt to taste

1 pound ground beef

2 jalapeños, seeded and diced

1/2 onion, sliced

4-5 garlic cloves, peeled and chopped

4 medium tomatoes, seeded and diced

8 green olives, pitted and sliced into quarters

2 tablespoons olive liquid

1/4 cup raisins (softened by soaking in warm water 20 minutes)

1 green bell pepper, seeded and chopped

1 teaspoon cumin

1/4 teaspoon ground cloves

1 small cone piloncillo, broken into pieces

- Prepare the potatoes.

- In a large skillet, cook the ground beef, jalapeños, onion, and garlic over medium heat until the beef is about halfway cooked.

- Add remaining ingredients; cook over low heat until the ingredients are evenly cooked.

- Fold in the roasted potatoes and serve immediately.

Delicious Vegetable Additions: There are a host of ingredients that can be added to your picadillo to create a delicious dish. You can add up to a cup of each of the following vegetables for a total of 2 cups: peas; carrots, peeled and julienned; potatoes, cubed; chayote squash, peeled and cubed. You can also add ¹/₂ cup of one the following: white wine, tomato sauce, bitter orange juice.

Additional Flavors: Add two or three of the following: 1 tablespoon capers; 1 chipotle chile canned in adobo sauce; 2 tablespoons white vinegar; 1 teaspoon tamarind paste; ¹/₂ teaspoon ground nutmeg; 1 sprig epazote; 2 to 3 bay leaves. If you use bay leaves, remove them before serving.

Prepare the Potatoes

- Place the potatoes in a medium bowl and toss with oil until evenly coated.

- Arrange potatoes in a single layer on a greased baking sheet and lightly sprinkle with salt.

- Place in a 350°F oven and bake about 30 minutes or until golden and cooked through.

- Use a spatula to flip the potatoes occasionally so they cook evenly.

Cooking the Picadillo

- Begin to brown the ground beef in a large pan over medium heat.

- Use a wooden spoon to separate and break up the ground beef as it cooks. Drain off excess fat as necessary.

- Fold in the ingredients one at time so they are evenly distributed.

- If the mixture seems dry, add ¼ cup water to moisten while cooking.

SHREDDED PORK ADOBADA

Pork simmered in a flavorful chile sauce makes a delicious meal or filling

Adobo is a classic Mexican marinade made with a mixture of chiles and seasonings. It is usually used to marinate pork and is sometimes used to marinate chicken. You can also find chipotle chiles marinated in adobo sold in cans at your local grocery store.

This aromatic marinade is generally not overly spicy but focuses more on the layers of flavors provided by the ingredients. Recipes for pork adobada vary by the ingredients in the sauce, as well as by the way the pork is cooked and served. This recipe features classic Mexican ingredients, and you can enjoy it as a main dish or as a delicious filling for tacos and burritos. *Yield: Serves 6*

Ingredients

4 ancho chiles, stems and seeds removed

2 guajillo chiles, stems and seeds removed

¹/₂ small onion, chopped

2 garlic cloves, crushed

1 tablespoon cooking oil

¹/₂ cup vinegar

1 cup orange juice

2 tablespoons lime juice

1 tablespoon dried oregano

2 bay leaves

1 teaspoon achiote paste

¹/₂ teaspoon ground cumin

1 teaspoon black pepper

¹/₂ teaspoon ground cinnamon

1 teaspoon salt

4 pounds boneless pork butt, cut into 3-inch chunks

1 quart water, as necessary

Shredded Pork Adobada

- Soak chiles 30 minutes in hot water to soften; reserve ½ cup soaking liquid. Blend or process chiles with soaking liquid until smooth.

- Sauté onion and garlic in oil over medium heat, 3 minutes. Add chiles, remaining ingredients except pork; simmer 20 minutes.

- Let the marinade cool. Place pork in a glass dish, pour marinade over the pork, and refrigerate 24 hours.

- Place pork and remaining marinade into a large pot. The liquid should cover the pork. Simmer 3 hours uncovered.

Grilled Pork Adobada: Another way to cook Pork Adobada is to grill it. You need to have the pork cut into thin slices about ¹/₂-inch thick. Marinate as directed. Heat the grill to medium heat and grill the marinated pork, using the remaining marinade to baste the pork during the first half of cooking.

Canned Chile Sauce: You can substitute canned red chile sauce if dried chiles are unavailable. Use 2 cups red chile sauce instead of the chiles and prepare the recipe as directed. You can also use lemon juice instead of lime juice.

Selecting the Pork

Simmering Pork Adobada

PORK DISHES

- You need only half a boneless pork butt, which is approximately 4 pounds; small variations are okay. Trim off excess fat.

- Pork butt comes from the shoulder area and may have the word SHOULDER on the package.

- If you purchase pork butt prepackaged, it should not contain any added water, salt, or other additives. Look for natural cuts, or purchase from your butcher to ensure quality meat.

- If you can't find boneless, cut the bone out when you cut the pork into chunks.

- Start with a large, cool pot, as the marinade might burn if you add it to a preheated pot.

- Add the pork and remaining marinade. You want enough liquid to cover the pork, so add additional water if necessary.

- You want the liquids to cook down slowly, creating a thickened sauce. If the liquid cooks off before the pork is ready, add more water.

- When the pork is ready, use 2 forks to shred it into bite-size pieces.

SLOW-ROASTED PORK

Slow roasting pork makes this inexpensive meat fork-tender and mouthwateringly good

Pork is enjoyed throughout the world, with its delicious flavor, easy accessibility, and variety of cuts. It is also inexpensive, which makes it a great choice for cooks on a budget.

Pork is widely used throughout Mexico in traditional recipes that date back hundreds of years. However, pork is not a native Mexican ingredient. It was brought over with the Spanish and quickly became part of the Mexican diet. Mexicans utilize the entire pig, from the cheeks to the feet.

Because certain cuts of pork can be tough or dry, they need a lengthy cooking time to become moist and tender. Slow roasting is an easy method, and the pork will be juicy and delicious. *Yield: Serves 4–6*

Slow-Roasted Pork

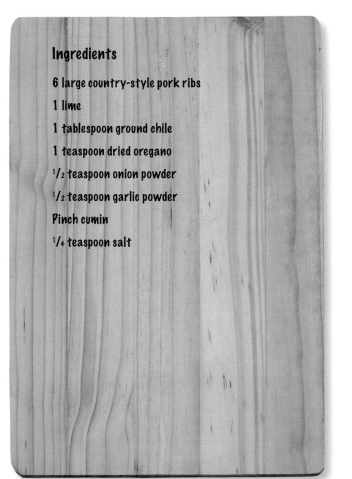

Ingredients

6 large country-style pork ribs

1 lime

1 tablespoon ground chile

1 teaspoon dried oregano

1/2 teaspoon onion powder

1/2 teaspoon garlic powder

Pinch cumin

1/4 teaspoon salt

- Rinse the pork briefly under cool water and pat dry.

- Cut the lime in half and squeeze the juice over the pork and rub it in.

- Combine remaining ingredients and rub onto the pork.

- Bake pork in a 300°F oven 2 hours covered and 1 hour uncovered.

Country-style pork ribs are cut from the blade end of the sirloin near the shoulder and do not contain bones. They do have a lot of fat, however, which should be trimmed before cooking. You can find country-style pork ribs as a slab, but more often it is cut into thick strips, and that's what you need for this recipe. Have your butcher cut the slab accordingly.

Reheating Leftovers: You can use leftover Slow-Roasted Pork in other dishes such as tortas, soup, or scrambled eggs. Reheat the pork by steaming it to keep it moist. Shred the pork into bite-size pieces, put it in small pot, and add 2 tablespoons water. Cover the pot and heat over medium-low heat, stirring occasionally until the water has evaporated and pork is hot.

Rub in Spices

- During the first hour of cooking, it's okay if liquid appears in the bottom of the baking dish. It will cook off as the pork roasts.

- Keep the pork loosely covered with foil to prevent the outside from drying out.

- After you uncover the pork, occasionally spoon liquid and fat over the meat to keep it moist.

- After 3 hours you should be able to easily cut into the pork with a spoon. If not, cook an additional 30 minutes.

Roasting and Serving Pork

- Serve Slow-Roasted Pork directly out of the baking dish, or drain it on paper towels to absorb any excess fat.

- Slow-Roasted Pork makes a delicious main dish served with rice and beans or a refreshing salad.

- You can also break the pork into bite-size chunks and use it to make tacos or burritos.

- Serve the pork immediately for best flavor and tenderness. As it cools it can dry out a bit and the outside can become somewhat tough.

CARNITAS

Moist and delicious pork that is slow-cooked and then browned in its own fat

Mexican peasants were often given the leftover cuts of meat after the wealthy landowners took the best parts. Carnitas, or "little meats," were cooked in a way that made the tougher, less desirable cuts of pork into a delicious meal. Carnitas can be made with a wide variety of cuts of pork, but the most common is the pork butt, which is actually from the shoulder

area of the pig. Pork butt is great for carnitas because it is well marbled and very flavorful.

Slow cooking the meat creates a wonderfully moist and silky texture with bits of crispiness on the outside. It makes a succulent main dish but is more often used as a filling for tacos. *Yield: Serves 6*

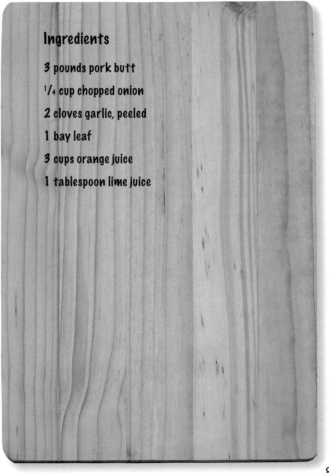

Ingredients

3 pounds pork butt

$^1/_4$ cup chopped onion

2 cloves garlic, peeled

1 bay leaf

3 cups orange juice

1 tablespoon lime juice

Carnitas

- Cut the pork into 3- to 4-inch chunks and place in a large pot along with the remaining ingredients.

- Cover and simmer 1 hour over low heat.

- Remove the cover and let the remaining liquid simmer until the liquid has cooked off and only the pork fat remains.

- Remove the bay leaf and shred the pork into bite-size pieces. Let it continue to cook in its own fat until the edges become brown and crispy. Drain and serve.

• • • • RECIPE VARIATIONS • • • •

Carnitas Made with Milk: Simmer the pork in milk instead of orange juice. This creates a creamy sauce that coats each piece and adds a subtle milk flavor.

Cola Carnitas: Use cola instead of orange juice or use a combination of the two. This adds a sweet flavor.

• • • • • • • • • YELLOW ◗ LIGHT • • • • • • • • • •

The key to Carnitas is the evaporation of the liquid, which leaves the fat behind. If the liquid cooks off too fast, cooking time is reduced and the pork isn't as tender. Add water if necessary to keep the liquid at the correct level. The liquid should have evaporated about halfway through the cooking time, after about 2 hours. If it is not cooking off fast enough, increase the heat a little at a time until the liquid is evaporating in the correct amount.

Simmering the Pork

- If the heat is low enough, the liquid should keep the pork covered during the first hour of cooking.

- If the liquid evaporates too quickly, add just enough water to replace what has cooked off.

- After removing the lid, the liquid should take about 2 hours to cook off, leaving behind the pork and fat.

- If the liquid cooks off too quickly, the pork won't have adequate time to become tender. Check often to make sure the liquid does not evaporate too quickly.

Browning the Pork

- After the liquid has cooked off, there will be a layer of fat on the bottom of the pot. This is just enough to brown the pork. Remove the bay leaf and discard.

- Use 2 forks to shred each piece of pork into bite-size pieces. Turn the pieces

often, allowing all edges to become crispy.

- Do not overcook the chunks; you don't want them browned all over, just the edges.

- Serve Carnitas with a slotted spoon or drain on paper towels before serving.

POC-CHUC

Tender grilled pork smothered with a spicy tomato sauce

Most Yucatan dishes bear no resemblance to the Mexican food that is known outside of the country. The region's tropical climate provides ingredients unique to the area and steeped in ancient culture. Most dishes cooked in this region are made from fresh and local ingredients, which lend to the rich flavors.

Before modern refrigeration, salt water was commonly used to preserve meat. Strong, acidic flavors were used to mask the saltiness, such as sour orange and vinegar. Even though preservation no longer requires salt, the signature flavors of poc-chuc remain.

The traditional way to cook poc-chuc is to let it cook over fiery embers, but with this recipe you can grill it in your own backyard. *Yield: Serves 6*

Ingredients

6 boneless pork steaks or 6 pieces pork tenderloin

1 tablespoon achiote paste

1 1/2 cups bitter orange juice, divided

3 teaspoons salt

1/2 teaspoon white pepper

Chiltomate

3 onions

2 tablespoons cooking oil.

1/2 teaspoon coriander

1 teaspoon vinegar

1/2 ounce piloncillo

1/4 teaspoon salt

Poc-Chuc

- Rinse the pork and pat it dry. Trim off any excess fat or membranes and discard.

- Place the pork in a large bowl and rub the achiote paste over it. Add 1 cup orange juice, salt, and pepper and cover the bowl. Refrigerate 24 hours.

- Heat grill to medium heat and cook the pork until it is done and no longer pink. Baste it with 1/2 cup orange juice during the cooking process. Meanwhile, prepare the onion topping.

- Top each piece of pork with the Chiltomate and onion topping. Serve immediately.

Chiltomate: Roast 4 large tomatoes, 1 habañero chile, and 1 onion, peeled and halved, on a grill over high heat; turn them frequently until they begin to char. Peel the tomatoes and chiles and remove the seeds. Combine the tomatoes, chile, onion, 1 bunch fresh cilantro, 1 tablespoon vinegar, 3 peeled garlic cloves, 2 tablespoons lime, and salt to taste in a food processor or blender; process or blend until smooth.

Grill the Poc-Chuc

- Lightly baste the pork every 5 minutes with orange juice.

- If you don't have bitter orange juice, substitute with ½ cup orange juice and ½ cup lime juice.

- Do not overcook the pork or it will lose moisture and dry out. It is ready when it is no longer pink in the center.

- A long, slow grilling time is important to help the pork stay moist and juicy.

Prepare Onion Topping

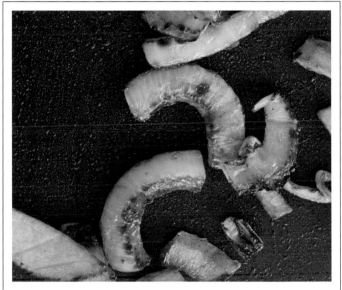

- Slice the onions and sauté in cooking oil.

- Cook the onions 10 minutes, or until softened. Sprinkle in coriander.

- Reduce heat and add vinegar, piloncillo, and salt.

- Cook an additional 5 minutes, until the onions begin to turn golden.

PORK IN CHILE SAUCE

This delicious shredded pork is fried with chiles, onions, and spices

Pork in chile sauce, or chilorio, is a pork dish with origins in the northern Mexican state of Sinaloa, where it is a thick rich stew of pork and pasilla chiles.

It is made by simmering pork in water until it is fork-tender and then frying pieces of the shredded pork in lard with chiles, onions, and spices. It can be found in canned form, but it tastes much better when made fresh.

Chilorio is primarily used as a filling for tacos or tamales and is sometimes served as a main dish. It is highly seasoned, and the flavors are very concentrated. *Yield: Serves 6*

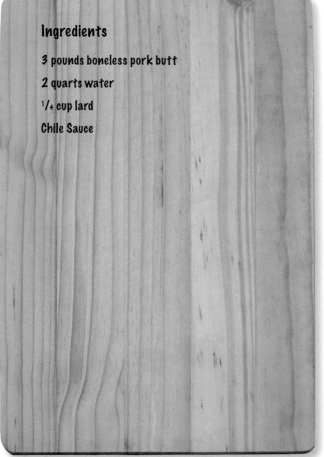

Ingredients

3 pounds boneless pork butt

2 quarts water

$1/4$ cup lard

Chile Sauce

Pork in Chile Sauce

- Place the pork into a large pot and add the water. Bring to a boil and then reduce to a simmer.

- Simmer the pork 2 hours; remove it from the pot and shred it.

- Heat a large pan over medium heat and melt the lard. Add the shredded pork and fry until it begins to get crispy.

- Add the Chile Sauce and continue to cook over medium heat 2 minutes. Serve Immediately.

Chile Sauce: Soak 3 to 4 ancho chiles, stems and seeds removed, in hot water until they are softened. In a medium-hot pan, heat 1 tablespoon lard until it melts. Add ½ onion, 3 garlic cloves, ½ teaspoon cumin, 1 tablespoon oregano, and 1 teaspoon salt. Cook 5 minutes or until the onions become soft and translucent. Let the ingredients cool; grind them into a thick sauce or use a food processor.

Shredding the Pork

- The pork should be fork-tender before you remove it to be shredded.

- Because it will be very hot, use 2 forks to tear the meat. Be careful of the steam that may be released from the meat as you shred it.

- If the pork has time to cool slightly, shred it by pulling it apart with your fingers.

- You can use a knife to coarsely chop the pork; the meat will shred as you cut it.

Frying the Pork

- Make sure the lard is ready before frying the meat. It is ready when a small piece of pork dropped into it sizzles.

- Because the pork and Chile Sauce both have moisture, be careful of the hot lard splatter when you place the meat and sauce into the pan.

- Fry the meat briefly, as you don't want it to dry out. As soon as the edges begin to get slightly crispy, it is time to add the Chile Sauce.

PORK DISHES

CHILE VERDE
A zesty stew made with chunks of pork, green chiles, and tomatillos

Chile verde or "green chile" is a rich and hearty stew with succulent chunks of tender pork simmered in a tangy green sauce made with tomatillos and green chiles. These two main ingredients are native to Mexico and were already being used to flavor dishes long before pork was imported. Even though there is no documentation as to the origins of chile verde, the dish was probably conceived while using green chile and tomatillos to flavor the pork, and eventually it evolved into a stew.

Chile verde is a straightforward dish and very easy to make. Even if measurements were not followed perfectly, it would probably still be a great dish. *Yield: Serves 4–6*

Ingredients

3 tablespoons oil

1 1/2 pounds boneless pork loin, cut into 2-inch cubes

2 cups chicken broth

1 cup green chile sauce

1 medium onion, peeled and diced

4 garlic cloves, peeled and diced

2 cups tomatillos, husks removed and coarsely chopped

2 poblano chiles, roasted

1/4 teaspoon black pepper

1/2 teaspoon salt

1/2 teaspoon cumin

1/2 teaspoon sugar

Chile Verde

- Heat oil in a skillet over high heat; quickly brown the outside of the pork.

- Pour the broth and chile sauce into a large pot and bring to a boil.

- Add the pork, onion, garlic, and tomatillos; simmer 2 hours over low heat. Meanwhile, roast the chiles.

- Add the chiles and let them simmer another hour. The liquid should reduce to a thin sauce. Season with pepper, salt, cumin, and sugar.

The type of chile used in this recipe plays an important role in the flavor of the final dish. The dark green poblano has a fresh, grassy flavor with mild heat. The light green hatch chile has an earthier taste with medium heat. If you can't locate fresh green chiles, substitute with canned, which are already roasted and peeled and ready to use.

Chicken Chile Verde: Use boneless, skinless chicken breast in place of the pork. Other parts of the chicken can be used, too, but be sure to remove the skin, bones, excess fat, and gristle.

Roast the Chiles

Simmering the Chile Verde

- Char the chiles under a broiler, on a grill, or on a hot comal until they are blackened and blistered.

- Place in an airtight plastic bag a few minutes. The steam will help loosen the skin further.

- Peel off the charred skin. You can run them under cold water to remove any remaining bits of skin.

- Cut the stem off each chile and slit it down the side. Use a spoon to scrape out the seeds.

- Keep the Chile Verde at a slow, steady simmer. Do not allow it to boil.

- If too much liquid cooks off and the pork still needs more time to cook, add water to replace what has evaporated.

- Stir occasionally to keep anything from sticking to the bottom of the pot.

- When the Chile Verde is ready, it should be a stew-like consistency. If it is too thin, it may need more time to simmer.

HUACHINANGO A LA VERACRUZANA

Also known as red snapper, this dish is marinated and then baked in a tangy tomato sauce

Huachinango is a popular fish in Mexico, found off the Pacific Coast and the Gulf of Mexico. Huachinango are also known as red snapper because of their light red color, which comes from the amount of shrimp they consume as a food source.

Red snapper is a type of rockfish, and when they are not available, other rockfish are sometimes used in this recipe.

They are generally cooked and served whole, but can also be filleted. Huachinango is a popular seafood choice in the state of Veracruz, which lies on the Gulf of Mexico. To prepare it as they do in Veracruz, the recipe includes tomatoes, capers, and green olives—some of the signature flavors of that region. *Yield: Serves 4*

Ingredients

3 pounds snapper fillets

3 tablespoons cooking oil

1 onion, sliced

2 garlic cloves, peeled and chopped

3 tomatoes, seeded and coarsely chopped

1/2 cup tomato sauce

1 bay leaf

1 teaspoon dried oregano

5 jalapeños (canned), roughly chopped

2 tablespoons capers

10 green olives, quartered

Huachinango a la Veracruzana

- Place the fish in a baking dish and pour marinade over the fillets. Refrigerate 1 hour.

- To make the sauce, heat the oil in a saucepan over medium heat; sauté the onion and garlic until the onion is translucent.

- Add remaining ingredients, except the fish; simmer 10 minutes.

- Drain the marinade off the fish and replace it with the sauce. Bake covered 30 minutes at 300°F. Remove the bay leaf before serving.

Marinade: Cut 2 large fresh limes in half and squeeze the juice into a small bowl. Peel 2 to 3 garlic cloves, chop them, and then stir them into the lime juice. Sprinkle a pinch of nutmeg, salt, and pepper over the top and then whisk all the ingredients together until well combined.

Selecting the Snapper

- For delicious results it is imperative that you choose fresh fish.

- Choose fillets that are translucent and have a pinkish tone.

- The fillets should be firm to the touch and in one piece. There should be no tears or pieces missing.

- The snapper should have a mild fish aroma. If the scent is overly fishy, the freshness is questionable.

Simmering the Sauce

- Make sure you start with a saucepan big enough to hold all the ingredients for the sauce.

- Preheat the pan over medium-high heat for 1 minute before adding the onion and garlic.

- Add the tomato sauce carefully, as it may splatter when you add it to the hot pan.

- The sauce is ready when the tomatoes have started to cook down and release their juices.

SEAFOOD DISHES

CHIPOTLE TILAPIA
Smoky and spicy, this tilapia is moist and full of flavor

Tilapia, freshwater fish, are usually farm raised. Because of their fast growth rate, they are very low in mercury; but because of their vegetarian diet, they are low in omega-3 fatty acids. Tilapia raised in North America, South America, and Mexico are of the highest quality.

When jalapeños are left on the vine at the end of the growing season, they begin to turn red and shrivel. These red jalapeños are dried and smoked to become chipotle chiles. Chipotle chiles are often soaked in adobo sauce and canned. The delicious smoky flavor of the chipotle combined with the tangy flavors of the sauce are a delicious complement to the mild flavor and flaky texture of tilapia. *Yield: Serves 4–6*

Ingredients

2 chipotle chiles canned in adobo sauce

2 tablespoons adobo sauce from canned chipotles

2 limes

2 garlic cloves, crushed

6 tilapia fillets

Chipotle Tilapia

- Chop the chipotle chiles. Combine the chopped chipotles and the adobo sauce in a bowl.

- Cut the limes in half and add the juice and garlic to the chipotle chiles.

- Place the tilapia into a glass baking dish and coat with the marinade. Cover and refrigerate 30 minutes.

- Cook the tilapia on a grill over medium heat until cooked through.

Fresh, locally grown tilapia is the best choice. The flesh should be white and firm. The skin should be bright and shiny and resume its shape if pressed. Tilapia may have a mild fish odor, but overall it should smell fresh and clean. Frozen tilapia is also available, but it's harder to determine the quality and may be imported from a questionable source. Buy fresh whenever possible.

• • • • RECIPE VARIATION • • • •

Ajo-Chile Tilapia Marinade: Peel and chop 2 garlic cloves. Thinly slice 1 scallion, discarding the root area. Combine the garlic and onion in a bowl and whisk in a pinch of salt, $1/4$ teaspoon chile powder, 1 tablespoon olive oil, and the juice of 1 lemon. Follow recipes as directed.

Preparing the Marinade

Grilling the Tilapia

- Rinse the tilapia under cold water and pat dry before marinating.

- Chipotles in adobo sauce can stain, so take care not to let the liquid splatter while you are chopping them—or wear an apron.

- If the adobo sauce is too thick, add 2 tablespoons water to thin the marinade.

- When you cut the limes, squeeze them over your hands so that any seeds are caught in your fingers.

- Make sure to oil the grates on the grill to prevent sticking.

- Heat the grill over medium-high heat. Place tilapia directly over the heat.

- Let each side cook for 2 to 3 minutes for smaller fillets and 4 minutes for larger pieces.

- Turn the fillets once halfway through the full cooking time so that they cook evenly. Do not turn them too often or they may fall apart.

OAXACAN SEA BASS

Moist and flavorful sea bass served over vegetables and chorizo

Oaxaca is known both for its complicated Mole sauces as well as its simple dishes using local ingredients for the freshest taste possible. The region is geographically diverse with valleys, mountains, and coastline allowing a wide variety of ingredients. Chiles and squash are native Mexican ingredients and Oaxaca is known for its delicious varieties of Chorizo sausage.

Black Sea Bass is found in the Pacific as well as the Gulf of Mexico and is on many Mexican restaurant menus. It is a moist and tender white fish with a mild flavor. *Yield: Serves 4*

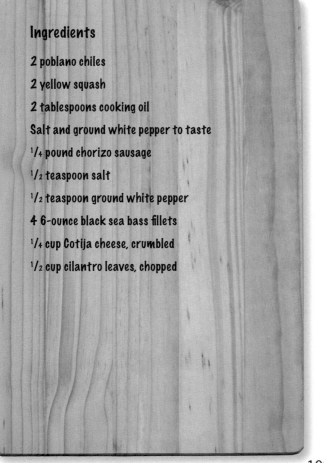

Ingredients

2 poblano chiles

2 yellow squash

2 tablespoons cooking oil

Salt and ground white pepper to taste

1/4 pound chorizo sausage

1/2 teaspoon salt

1/2 teaspoon ground white pepper

4 6-ounce black sea bass fillets

1/4 cup Cotija cheese, crumbled

1/2 cup cilantro leaves, chopped

Oaxacan Sea Bass

- Slice the chiles and squash, brush with oil, sprinkle with salt and pepper, and roast under a broiler 10 minutes, turning once. Remove skins from chiles. Set aside.

- Remove casing from chorizo and cook over medium heat until crumbled and well done. Set aside.

- Sprinkle the salt and pepper over the sea bass and panfry in the chorizo drippings over medium heat until done.

- Serve each fillet over the roasted vegetables and top with chorizo, Cotija, and cilantro.

Choosing fresh black sea bass is easy if you know what to look for. The fillet should be white, without dark spots or blemishes. It should have a mild ocean aroma, not a strong fishy smell. The skin should be shiny and intact. The flesh should feel firm to the touch and not soft or mushy.

Homemade Chorizo: Mix $1/4$ pound pork sausage with $1/2$ teaspoon chile powder, $1/4$ teaspoon garlic powder, $1/4$ teaspoon onion powder, 1 teaspoon dried oregano, $1/4$ teaspoon dried coriander, 1 teaspoon vinegar, $1/4$ teaspoon cayenne pepper, and a pinch of ground cloves. After ingredients are thoroughly combined, store in the refrigerator up to 48 hours.

Roasting the Vegetables

- Slice the yellow squash at an angle for a nice presentation. Make sure the slices are uniform.

- Cut the stems off of the chiles and use a spoon to scrape out the seeds and veins before roasting.

- Use a basting brush to apply a light coat of oil to each piece and then sprinkle with salt and pepper.

- Place them in a single layer on a baking sheet and broil until softened but not mushy.

Panfrying the Sea Bass

- Heat the drippings over medium-high heat before placing the fish into the pan.

- Let the fish sear on each side until it begins to turn brown and crispy on the edges.

- After searing the fish, turn the heat to medium low and cook 2 to 3 minutes on each side.

- The sea bass is done when it is no longer translucent, yet still moist on the inside.

SHRIMP CEVICHE

This cool and refreshing shrimp dish is made with fresh limes and lemons

Ceviche's origins lie in Central America, where the seafood is in abundance. Fresh fish and shrimp caught on a daily basis are often marinated in lime juice right on the boat or on the beach. The acid in the lime juice interacts with the proteins in the fish, giving the seafood a cooked texture. Back before the Spanish imported citrus fruits, the seafood was usually seasoned with chiles and salt and eaten raw.

Although ceviche is prepared in many Latin American countries, and the recipes vary from region to region, the basic preparation of marinating the seafood in citrus juice remains the same. In Mexico it is usually served with toasted corn tortillas or tortilla chips. *Yield: Serves 4*

Shrimp Ceviche

Ingredients

3 pounds small, fresh, raw shrimp, cleaned and de-veined

4 lemons

6 limes

4 large tomatoes, seeded and diced

$1/2$ cup cilantro leaves, chopped

1 serrano chile, seeded and finely chopped

$1/2$ cucumber, peeled and diced

1 red onion, peeled and chopped

Salt and pepper to taste

3 tablespoons tomato sauce

Lime wedges

- Lay the shrimp in a single layer in a glass baking dish or other nonreactive cookware.

- Cut the lemons and limes in half and squeeze the juice over the shrimp; refrigerate 3 hours.

- Remove the shrimp and place in a large bowl with the remaining ingredients (except the lime wedges), and toss the ingredients together.

- Refrigerate the mixture 1 hour and serve chilled and garnished with lime wedges.

YELLOW ● LIGHT

Shrimp can spoil very quickly, so if there is any question whether or not your shrimp is freshly caught, you will need to quickly cook them in boiling water 1 minute to make sure to destroy any bacteria that may be present. Place the cooked shrimp in a bowl of ice water to stop the cooking.

• • • • RECIPE VARIATION • • • •

Ceviche de Pescado: You can make ceviche with just about any high-quality fresh white fish: sea bass, tuna, mackerel, or red snapper. Cod and pollock have a slightly rubbery texture and are not suitable for ceviche. You need 3 pounds for this recipe. Cut the fish into bite-size pieces to replace the shrimp.

Marinating the Shrimp

- Make sure to give the shrimp a bit of space so they marinate evenly.

- Use a spoon to move the shrimp around in the juice to make sure they are evenly coated.

- The juice should be liberal enough to coat the shrimp and cover the bottom of the pan, but the shrimp should not be swimming in it.

- Use a spoon to pick up excess liquid and pour it over the shrimp to keep it moist.

Preparing the Ceviche

- Chop the vegetables into even-size pieces, about the size of a large pea.

- The shrimp is fully "cooked" when they are pinkish and opaque and have the texture of cooked shrimp.

- Toss the ingredients together carefully so as to not crush them.

- Ceviche is usually served cold with tortilla chips.

SEAFOOD DISHES

COCTEL DE CAMARÓN
This shrimp cocktail boasts succulent shrimp served in seasoned tomato juice

Coctel de camarón (shrimp cocktail) is found on the menu in just about every region of Mexico. Unlike the American versions of small shrimp served with a thick cocktail sauce, coctel de camarón is served almost like a beverage in a large, tall glass with enormous, succulent shrimp swimming in a delicious liquid of tomatoes and seasonings. Some restaurants make a specialty of coctel de camarón, and the locals enjoy it on a daily basis.

Choosing large fresh shrimp is imperative to a delicious and authentic coctel de camarón. Use the freshest produce available for the best flavor. *Yield: Serves 2*

Ingredients

1 cup tomato sauce

1 cup chilled poaching liquid

$1/2$ teaspoon coriander

$1/2$ teaspoon sugar

$1/2$ teaspoon salt

2 tablespoons white vinegar

$1/4$ teaspoon hot chile sauce

16 large shrimp, poached, peeled, and chilled

$1/4$ cup finely chopped cucumber

$1/4$ cup finely chopped onion

$1/4$ cup finely chopped celery

1 plum tomato, seeded and diced

1 cup cilantro leaves, chopped

Celery stalk with leaves (optional)

Lime wedges (optional)

1 avocado (optional)

Coctel de Camarón

- In a large bowl whisk together the tomato sauce and poaching liquid.

- Add the coriander, sugar, salt, vinegar, and chile sauce. Cover and refrigerate 30 minutes.

- Place 8 shrimp into two glasses.

- Stir the chopped vegetables and cilantro into the tomato mixture and pour over the shrimp to fill each glass.

Poached Shrimp: Combine 2 quarts water; 3 peeled garlic cloves; 1 onion, peeled and cut in half; 3 jalapeños, stems and seeds removed; and 1 bay leaf in a large pot and bring to a boil. Turn the heat to low and add 16 large shrimp in the shell and the juice of 1 lemon. Simmer 5 to 6 minutes or until shrimp are pink and begin to curl. Use a slotted spoon to remove the shrimp from the liquid. Peel the shrimp, then cover and refrigerate to chill. Reserve 1 cup poaching liquid.

Preparing the Coctel

- You want the tomato sauce and poaching liquid mixture to be slightly watery. Add more water by the tablespoon to achieve a thin consistency.

- Add seasonings and adjust salt to taste.

- The hot chile sauce should add just a touch of heat, so choose one that is not too overpowering.

- The seasonings need time to flavor the sauce, so a minimum of 30 minutes in the refrigerator is necessary, but you can also leave it overnight.

Assembling Coctel de Camarón

- Add the vegetables to the tomato mixture just before serving so they stay crisp.

- When you pour the sauce into the glass, stir it slightly to distribute the shrimp throughout the liquid.

- If desired, add a stalk of celery to each glass. The stalk can also be used to eat the shrimp, but you should also provide spoons.

- You can also garnish with a slice or two of avocado placed on top and a lime wedge on the rim.

CAMARÓN DEL DIABLO

This fiery shrimp dish gets its flavor from ancho chiles, garlic, and lime

Shrimp is a popular seafood, especially along the coastal regions of Mexico. The shrimp caught along the tropical coast are usually large and meaty with a subtle sweetness and a soft texture. They are enjoyed myriad ways, but Camarón del Diablo is a delicious way to taste the flavors of Mexico.

Ancho chiles, which are dried poblano chiles, have a rich,

raisin flavor, and the chiles de arbol add a punch of heat that gives this dish the name, which translate to "devil's shrimp." The onions and garlic round out the flavors, and cooking the shrimp on the grill adds another layer of smoky flavor.
Yield : Serves 2–3

Ingredients

2 ancho chiles, dried

1 chile de arbol, dried

1/2 cup tomato sauce

4 garlic cloves, peeled and crushed

1/4 cup chopped onion

1 lime, juiced

1 teaspoon white vinegar

2 tablespoons cooking oil

1/4 teaspoon salt (or more to taste)

25 large frozen shrimp, thawed, shelled and cleaned

1 green onion, chopped

Camarón del Diablo

- Cut the stems off of the dried chiles and slit them down the side. Shake them to remove the seeds.

- Soak the chiles in hot water 30 minutes. Reserve ½ cup soaking liquid.

- In a blender, puree the chiles, tomato sauce, garlic, onion, lime juice, vinegar, oil, and salt into a sauce.

- Place 5 shrimp on each skewer; baste with sauce. Grill over medium heat until done.

Turn Down the Heat: While Camarón del Diablo is meant to be extremely spicy, you can tone down the heat by eliminating the chile de arbol which is the greatest source of heat. The Ancho chiles are a bit spicy on their own so you will still have some fiery flavor without being overpowering.

Fresh Fare: If you have it available, fresh shrimp is delicious in this recipe as well. Make sure to clean them well and remove the heads and/or legs if necessary. You may also need to de-vein and clean them. Once they are prepared, cook them immediately.

Preparing the Skewers

- Frozen shrimp deteriorates very quickly after it thaws out, so don't defrost them until right before you are ready to grill.

- If you are using wooden skewers, soak them 30 minutes in warm water to prevent them from scorching.

- Slide the shrimp onto the skewer head end first and then slide the skewer through the portion just before the tail.

- Use a basting brush to evenly coat the shrimp with sauce.

Grilling the Shrimp

- Lightly oil the grilling surface. Heat the grill to medium heat.

- When the grill is sufficiently hot, quickly lay the skewers on to cook about 4 minutes.

- Turn the shrimp and baste them every minute or so. They are done when they become opaque and begin to curl.

- Serve shrimp over a bed of rice and top with a sprinkle of sliced green onion.

SEAFOOD DISHES

AUTHENTIC GUACAMOLE

A traditional preparation of avocado with tomatoes and onions creates a delicious dip and topping

The origins of guacamole go all the way back to the Aztecs, who prepared avocados in much the same way we do today by mashing them and then adding other ingredients. They believed avocados were an aphrodisiac, and the fruit was prized for its fat and protein content because the Aztecs had a naturally low-fat diet.

The Aztecs love of the avocado led to the invading Spaniards becoming quite smitten with the fruit, and they attempted to bring it back to Europe. Unfortunately the avocados did not grow well in the European climate and guacamole became an exotic food to be enjoyed in tropical locations. *Yield: Serves 4–6*

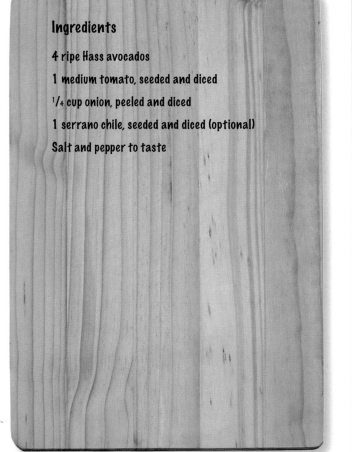

Ingredients

4 ripe Hass avocados

1 medium tomato, seeded and diced

1/4 cup onion, peeled and diced

1 serrano chile, seeded and diced (optional)

Salt and pepper to taste

Authentic Guacamole

- Cut each avocado in half and remove the seed. Scoop the avocado flesh out of the skin with a large spoon.

- Place the avocado in a bowl and mash with a plastic spatula until it is somewhat smooth with some small chunks.

- Add the remaining ingredients on top of the mashed avocado and fold them in. Adjust the amount of chile you use to your taste.

- Serve the guacamole immediately with your favorite corn chips or use it as a topping.

The most common type of avocado grown in the United States is the Hass variety, which just happens to be ideal for making a delicious guacamole. They are medium-size with a teardrop shape and have a smooth, creamy texture. As the avocado grows, the skin is deep green at first and, as the avocado ripens, becomes black. They are available in most markets year-round.

MAKE IT EASY

Avocado flesh quickly oxidizes and turns gray when exposed to air, so it can be a challenge to make guacamole ahead of time. Prepare the other ingredients ahead of time and place them in a large, covered bowl. Right before you are ready to serve it, slice the avocados open, remove the seed, and add them to the other ingredients, using a rubber spatula to slice and mash the avocados.

Removing the Seed

- Avocados are easy to work with if you know a few tricks. Ripened avocados are easiest to work with.

- Slice the avocado lengthwise, cutting around the large seed.

- Twist the halves slightly until one side breaks away.

- Carefully use a butcher knife to quickly and firmly "tap" the seed. The knife should go about ⅛ inch into the seed.

- Using the butcher knife as a handle, carefully twist out the seed and discard.

Preparing the Guacamole

- The ingredients will be combined when you mash them together with the avocado, so make sure they are evenly distributed.

- Some lumps are okay, but the final guacamole should be fairly smooth.

- Serve the guacamole as soon as possible, as it will begin to turn brown when it is exposed to air.

- Serve Authentic Guacamole with crunchy tortilla chips or use it to top your favorite tacos or tostadas.

CLASSIC GUACAMOLE

This delicious topping and dip has a creamy texture and a slight kick of heat from the chile sauce

Avocados have long been valued by native Mexicans for their nutritional content. But in more recent history, as low-fat diets were praised as the road to good health, avocados were frowned upon because they had a high fat content. One avocado can contain up to 30 grams of fat, which is the equivalent of a cheeseburger.

However, new light shed on these delicious fruits have proved that their fats are of the good variety and are actually good for you.

Use the guacamole as a topping for your favorite Mexican dish or a dip for your favorite tortilla chips. *Yield: Serves 3–4*

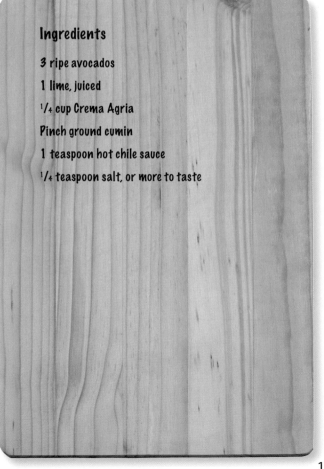

Ingredients

3 ripe avocados

1 lime, juiced

$1/4$ cup Crema Agria

Pinch ground cumin

1 teaspoon hot chile sauce

$1/4$ teaspoon salt, or more to taste

Classic Guacamole

- Cut the avocados in half and remove the seed by firmly tapping it with a butcher knife and twisting it out.

- Scrape the flesh out of the skin and place it into a bowl large enough to hold all the ingredients.

- Begin to mash the avocado. Add remaining ingredients and continue to mash them together.

- Guacamole is ready when the ingredients are well combined and it is fairly smooth.

Guacamole Sauce: For a delicious and beautiful green avocado sauce that you can drizzle over burritos, taquitos, or salads substitute $1/2$ cup Mexican crema for the Crema Agria . The crema has a thinner consistency and will make the guacamole more like a sauce than a dip.

Avocado oxidizes into a grayish color when it is exposed to air. While it is safe to consume, it is quite unappetizing when your guacamole turns gray. There are many methods purported to prevent the oxidation, such as lemon juice or keeping the pits in contact with the guacamole. The best method is to prevent air from reaching the guacamole with a layer of plastic wrap placed directly on its surface.

Ripening Avocados

- Ripened avocados are ideal for guacamole and can be used immediately.

- If hard, unripened avocados are all that's available, place them in a paper bag at room temperature for 3 to 5 days.

- Check the avocados daily, as they may ripen more quickly than you think.

- If the avocados ripen before you are ready to use them, place them in the fridge in an airtight container for up to a week.

Selecting Avocados

- Select avocados that are slightly soft under light finger pressure, but not overly mushy.

- Look for avocados that are even in tone without any dark spots or tears in the skin.

- The avocados should not have soft spots or areas where you can see that the skin is indented.

- When you cut the avocado open it should be a uniform light green color without any brown spots. Remove and discard any discolored areas.

GUACAMOLES & DIPS

GUACAMOLE POBLANO
Roasted poblano chiles add texture and flavor to this zesty dip

Poblano chiles are named after the Mexican state of Puebla, which is where they originated. They are popular because they are large and sturdy enough to be stuffed with fillings. They are also readily available, making them an easy choice when green chile is called for. Poblanos are usually 4 to 6 inches in length and dark green in color. The heat of a poblano can vary greatly from very mild to medium hot.

The poblano's combination of zesty flavors stands out against the mild flavor and creamy texture of the avocado. The Hass avocado is the best choice for this recipe, but Gwen or Bacon varieties can also be used. *Yield: Serves 4–6*

Ingredients

2 poblano chiles

3 large ripe Hass avocados

¹/₄ cup white onion, peeled and finely chopped

2 tablespoons lemon juice

2 teaspoons hot chile sauce

¹/₄ cup fresh cilantro, finely chopped

¹/₄ teaspoon salt, or more to taste

Guacamole Poblano

- Roast the poblanos under the broiler, on a hot comal, or on a grill until the skins are black.

- Remove the skin, stems, and seeds and finely dice the chiles.

- Cut the avocados in half, remove the seeds, and scrape the flesh into a bowl; begin to mash.

- Add remaining ingredients and continue to mash together until combined.

Look for chiles that are firm to the touch and even in color and texture. If heat level is a concern, there is no way to tell from the outside what it will be. Sometimes a grocer or farmer can advise you, but even that can be unreliable because everyone's heat perception is different. You can soak the chiles in cool water for 30 minutes to help reduce the heat level.

Fresh roasted chiles offer the best and most intense flavor for this guacamole. If you can't find fresh poblanos, use Anaheim chiles. If fresh chiles are not available, use 1 4-ounce can diced green chiles. Rinse them and pat them dry before adding to recipe, as you don't want any additional liquid in the guacamole.

Preparing the Poblanos

Serving the Guacamole

- Place the charred chiles into a small plastic bag to let them steam for a minute before removing the skins.

- You can hold them under running water to help remove any remaining bits of skin.

- After cutting the stem off, it should be easy to scrape out the seeds with a spoon. Don't worry if the chile tears while you are working with it.

- Cut the chile into long, thin strips and then cut the strips into smaller pieces.

- Guacamole needs to be served immediately to avoid its oxidizing and turning brown.

- If you need to postpone serving it, place a piece of plastic wrap over the container, touching the surface of the guacamole.

- Guacamole is usually served out of a bowl, but you can serve individual portions in fresh poblano chile halves.

- If the Guacamole begins to brown, just scrape off the discolored area and discard.

QUESO FUNDIDO

A tasty combination of melted cheese, spicy sausage, and roasted chile makes a great dip

Queso fundido is a crowd-pleaser to say the least. Just about everyone loves melted cheese, and when you add the flavors of zesty chorizo and tangy poblano chiles, you just can't go wrong. Set out a hot dish of this classic Mexican dip and watch it disappear.

The most common recipes for queso fundido usually require chorizo and chiles, but there are hundreds of varieties that call for ingredients such as mushrooms, garlic, tomatoes, salsa, or chile sauce. You can easily adjust any queso fundido recipe to suit your own taste.

Queso fundido is usually served with a bowl of fresh tortilla chips or a stack of piping-hot fresh tortillas. *Yield: Serves 6*

Ingredients

1 poblano chile

1/2 pound of Mexican chorizo

1 cup chopped onion

2 plum tomatoes, seeded and diced

3 cups shredded Manchego

1/4 cup Cotija, crumbled

12 flour or corn tortillas

Queso Fundido

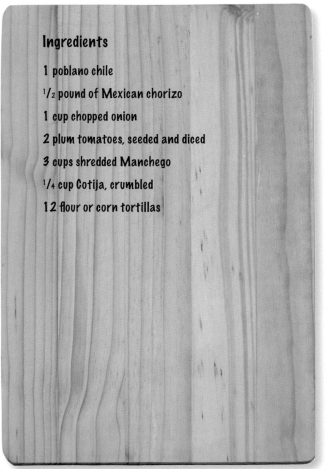

- Roast the chiles and remove the stem and seeds. Chop and set aside.

- Remove the casing from the chorizo and begin to brown it over medium heat. Add the onions; cook 5 minutes.

- Drain the fat off the chorizo mixture and add the chiles, tomatoes, and Manchego. Cook over medium heat until cheese melts, about 1 minute.

- Immediately transfer to a bowl and top with the Cotija.

You can make the poblano and chorizo mixture up to 24 hours in advance. Cook it as directed and let it cool completely before covering it and storing it in the refrigerator. When you are ready, reheat the mixture until it is hot and then follow the steps to add the cheese. The cheese doesn't hold well, so be sure to serve it immediately.

ZOOM

Mexican cheeses are usually available in your local supermarket. They may be in a different area than regular cheese, so be sure to ask if you can't find it. If you have a Mexican market nearby, you will find a variety of Mexican cheeses prepackaged or available by the pound. If you don't have Manchego available, a decent substitute is a good-quality Monterrey Jack.

Cooking the Chorizo

- Mexican chorizo is a soft sausage that can be browned similar to ground beef.

- Since the texture is quite soft, you will need to work the sausage while cooking it to make sure it cooks evenly and becomes crumbly.

- If the chorizo comes packaged in links, cut the end off of each link and squeeze it out into the pan.

- The onions won't take as long to cook as the chorizo, so add them when the chorizo is about halfway done.

Melting the Cheese

- Make sure to drain the excess fat from the chorizo so the dip will not be greasy.

- Make sure to remove most of the seeds and liquids when you chop the tomatoes, as excess liquid could cause the cheese to seize up and become rubbery.

- When you add the cheese, keep the ingredients moving so the cheese melts evenly and doesn't brown.

- Once the cheese has melted, immediately remove the mixture from the heat.

GUACAMOLES & DIPS

FIESTA BEAN DIP

This is a zesty and flavorful bean dip made with pinto beans and green chiles

Beans not only make a great side dish, they also make a delicious dip for your favorite corn tortilla chips. Pinto beans have a wonderful earthy flavor, and in this dip recipe they pair well with the fresh flavors of the salsa and tangy roasted green chiles.

Aztecs often used chiles to flavor their beans, and pairing those two ingredients is still an integral part of classic Mexican food. Modern versions of bean dips, with their simple ingredients, are probably prepared in much the same way beans were prepared hundreds of years ago. *Yield: Serves 8–10*

Ingredients

¼ cup lard or cooking oil

3 cups cooked pinto beans, drained

⅔ cup cooking liquid from beans

1 4-ounce can diced green chiles

1 cup fresh salsa

2 cups queso quesadilla, shredded

3 tablespoons sour cream

Fiesta Bean Dip

- In a large pot melt the lard and add the beans. Mash and fry the beans 3 minutes.

- Gradually stir in the cooking liquid to thin out the bean mixture.

- Fold in the chiles and salsa and simmer 2 minutes. Remove from heat and fold in the cheese.

- When the cheese is melted, transfer to a bowl and top with a dollop of sour cream.

Try Different Salsas: Experiment with different salsas in this recipe. For a mild, fresh flavor, use a chunky pico de gallo made with tomatoes, onions, and cilantro. For a smoky flavor with medium heat, go with a flavorful chipotle salsa. If you want to bring out the flavors of the green chiles, a salsa verde would be an excellent choice.

Substituting the Pinto Beans: If you don't have freshly cooked pinto beans on hand, use canned beans. Be sure to drain and reserve the liquid. Canned beans have a slightly slimy coating, so rinse them after draining. Take it one step further and use canned refried beans and skip the frying step. Although these shortcuts will save you time, there is a drawback: The dip won't be quite as flavorful.

Frying the Beans

- Make sure the lard or oil is very hot before adding the beans.

- As they fry in the oil, quickly mash the beans and then move them to the side of the pan to mash additional beans.

- Make sure the beans are drained well before adding them to the hot lard or the hot oil may splatter due to the excess liquid.

- Keep the heat at medium high to avoid scorching the beans.

Preparing the Dip

- You can use any salsa of your choice, but a chunkier style or pico de gallo works well to add texture.

- Drain excess liquids off the salsa so as to not water down the bean dip.

- Fold the cheese in and let it rest until it is melted. You want the cheese to be melted in the beans but not completely mixed.

- Serve the bean dip with your favorite tortilla chips.

CREAMY SALSA DIP

This appetizing dip combines the elements of fresh salsa with the tanginess of sour cream

Crema Agria is a type of Mexican sour cream that starts out as a heavy cream and then is fermented until it becomes even thicker and tart. It is creamier and richer than the traditional sour cream found in the United States and can be used in a variety of ways. The most common use for Crema Agria is as a topping to add a cool richness and tanginess to a dish.

Crema Agria's rich and creamy texture makes it the perfect base to create a mouthwatering dip that is quick and easy to prepare. Fresh ingredients such as ripe, juicy tomatoes and sweet green onions add delicious texture, while the cumin and ground chiles lend an earthy flavor. This scrumptious dip adds flair to any fiesta. *Yield: Serves 6-8*

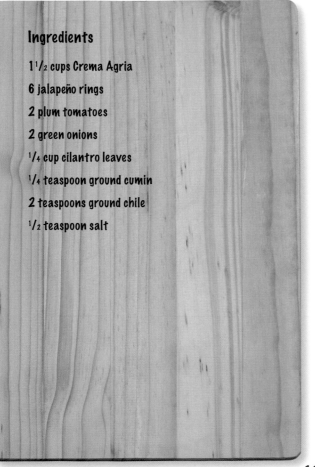

Ingredients

1 1/2 cups Crema Agria

6 jalapeño rings

2 plum tomatoes

2 green onions

1/4 cup cilantro leaves

1/4 teaspoon ground cumin

2 teaspoons ground chile

1/2 teaspoon salt

Creamy Salsa Dip

- Place the Crema Agria in a mixing bowl. Chop the jalapeños and add them to the bowl.

- Chop the tomatoes, discarding the seeds and liquid, and add them to the bowl.

- Slice the green onions at an angle and then add them to the bowl.

- Fold in the remaining ingredients and refrigerate 30 minutes before serving to let flavors combine.

Crema Agria: Warm 1 cup heavy cream over low heat until it is hot but not simmering. Gently stir in 2 table-spoons cultured buttermilk. Transfer the mixture to a jar and cover loosely. Let it stand at room temperature for 8 to 10 hours or until the mixture thickens. When it is the desired consistency, store it in the refrigerator.

Quick and Easy Creamy Salsa Dip: If you're short on time, substitute up to one cup of chunky salsa, such as a pico de gallo, for the tomatoes, onions, cilantro, and jalapeño. You may need to reduce the salt in the recipe, however, as many commercially prepared salsas have salt in them already. If the salsa is watery, try straining some of the liquid off so that the dip does not become too thin.

Preparing the Tomatoes

- Cut the tomato flesh away from the watery inner seed ball and discard the stem and seeds.

- Use your fingers to scrape off any excess liquid from the tomato pieces.

- Cut each piece of tomato into strips and then cross-wise to make small cubes.

- Fold the tomatoes into the dip; you don't want them to get mashed.

Making the Dip

- Prepare all the ingredients beforehand to make it easy to add them to the Crema Agria.

- Slice the green onions into thin pieces at an angle about ⅛-inch wide. You can reserve a few pieces to sprinkle on top as a garnish.

- You can prepare the vegetables up to 24 hours in advance and store them in the refrigerator.

- The dip needs to rest in order to enhance the flavors, so make it at least 30 minutes or up to to 12 hours in advance.

GUACAMOLES & DIPS

CHILES RELLENOS

Roasted green chiles that have been stuffed and fried in a simple batter is an authentic dish

Chiles rellenos translates to "stuffed chiles," and the dish originated in the lively city of Puebla, known for many signature Mexican dishes such as chiles en nogada and rompope.

Poblano chiles are named for the city of Puebla and are the most traditional chile to use for this recipe. The dark green, bulbous chiles are large and round and have plenty of room for fillings. Roasted chiles can easily develop tears, so the thick flesh of the poblano is ideal.

Queso fresco is a fresh Mexican cheese that holds its shape even when melted, which makes it an ideal filling for chiles rellenos. Queso blanco and panela, also fresh cheeses, are good substitutes for queso fresco. *Yield: Serves 4*

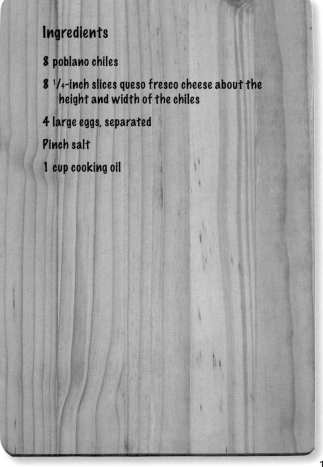

Ingredients

8 poblano chiles

8 ¼-inch slices queso fresco cheese about the height and width of the chiles

4 large eggs, separated

Pinch salt

1 cup cooking oil

Chiles Rellenos

- Char and peel the poblano chiles. Cut a small slit near the top of each chile and use a spoon to scrape out the seeds.

- Place a cheese slice into each chile.

- Whip the egg whites into stiff peaks and then fold in the yolks and salt until a batter forms.

- Dip each chile into the egg batter and fry in oil until golden. Drain each chile and serve immediately.

ZOOM

• • • • • RECIPE VARIATION • • • • •

Chile Rellenos with Picadillo Filling: While stuffing chiles rellenos with cheese is a simple and delicious way to make them, they are well suited to a large variety of fillings. Try beef picadillo, which is ground beef simmered with flavorful tomatoes, zesty onions, and tangy green olives for a whole new chile relleno experience.

Even though most green chiles are ready to pick at the end of summer, you can usually find them year-round. They are also easily grown in your own backyard and can be found at most farmer's markets. Look for chiles that are a uniform dark green color that are firm to the touch. They should not have any dark spots, dents, or tears, and they should be free of any mold or wrinkled skin.

Making the Batter

- Use a clean, cold mixing bowl to help keep the egg whites stiff.

- When you separate the eggs, do not let any yolk get into the whites, as the fats could prevent them from whipping into stiff peaks.

- Use a fork to mix the yolks and salt in a bowl, and then pour them over the egg whites.

- Gently fold the yolks into the whites, being careful to maintain some of the fluffiness of the egg whites.

Frying the Chiles

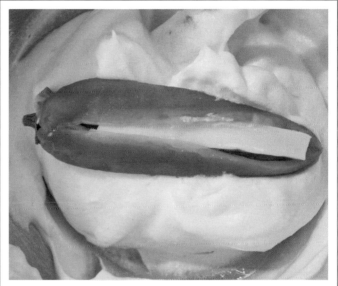

- Heat the oil in a saucepan over medium-high heat. When a drop of the egg batter sizzles and floats, the oil is ready.

- You want the oil ready before you begin dipping the chiles, as they need to be fried immediately.

- Fry the chile on each side for about 1 or 2 minutes, turning only once.

- Quickly remove chiles to a paper towel to absorb excess oil; serve immediately.

CHILES EN NOGADA

This is a unique dish of stuffed chiles topped with a creamy walnut sauce and pomegranate seeds

Originating from the city of Puebla, this tasty dish was developed by nuns in the early 1800s for Agustin de Iturbide, who helped gain Mexico's independence. The colors were meant to represent the colors of the Mexican flag, with the chile green, the sauce white, and the pomegranate red.

Chiles en nogada is a seasonal dish usually enjoyed during the month of September to celebrate Mexican independence. The dish consists of poblano chiles roasted and then stuffed with a savory and sweet picadillo filling. They are then smothered in a nutty walnut sauce, topped with fruity and crunchy pomegranate seeds, and served at room temperature. *Yield: Serves 6*

Ingredients

6 poblano chiles

$1/2$ pound ground pork

3 cloves garlic

$1/4$ cup white onion, chopped

1 green apple, peeled, cored, and chopped

$1/4$ cup crushed pineapple

2 tablespoons raisins, softened in warm water

$1/4$ teaspoon ground cinnamon

$1/4$ teaspoon ground nutmeg

$1/4$ teaspoon ground cumin

3 eggs, separated

Salt to taste

$1/2$ cup cooking oil

Walnut Sauce

1 pomegranate, seeds removed

1 bunch parsley

Chiles en Nogada

- Char and peel the poblano chiles. Cut a slit down the side and use a spoon to scrape out the seeds.

- Brown the pork with the garlic, onion, apple, pineapple, raisins, and seasonings.

- Whip the egg whites into stiff peaks, fold in the yolks and salt until a batter forms.

- Dip each chile in the batter and fry on each side until golden brown. Remove to serving plates; top with Walnut Sauce, pomegranate seeds, and parsley.

• • • • RECIPE VARIATIONS • • • •

Walnut Sauce: Tear ½ a bolillo roll into chunks and place it in a blender with 1 cup whole milk, ½ cup heavy cream, ¼ cup cream cheese, ½ pound shelled and peeled fresh walnuts, 1 tablespoon honey, a pinch cinnamon, and a pinch salt. The liquid should just cover the ingredients; add more milk if necessary. Pulse on high speed until sauce is smooth.

Walnut Skin: The light skin that covers the walnuts is brown and slightly bitter. The sauce is much better if you remove the skins from the walnuts; however, some people skip that step and leave the skins on.

Stuffing the Chiles

- When removing the seeds from the chiles, be careful not to tear the flesh.

- Let the filling cool slightly before attempting to stuff the chiles.

- Hold each chile in your hand with the slit side up and carefully spoon in the filling. Gently squeeze the chile to help close it.

- You want just enough filling to fill out the chile; don't overstuff it.

Preparing the Walnuts for the Sauce

- Choose fresh walnuts that are slightly green. Crack each nut open and remove the nutmeat.

- Boil 3 quarts water. Place a small batch of walnut meat into the boiling water for just a few seconds and remove.

- Use your fingers to peel off the brown skin and use a nut pick tool to get into the crevices.

- Fresh walnuts will peel very easily, while older ones will be more difficult.

RAJAS CON CREMA

A simple dish of roasted chiles and onions and finished in a cream sauce

Rajas in their simplest form are strips of roasted green chiles. However, most varieties include other aromatic vegetables, as well as seasonings. Sometimes a cream or Crema Agria is added, which gives them a silky texture.

Rajas are not really a main dish but are used as a filling for other items such as tacos and burritos. They are also served as a side dish for chicken or beef. They are traditionally made with fresh roasted green chiles, but you can substitute canned roasted green chiles in a pinch.

Poblano chiles are usually used to make rajas, but you can use your favorite green chile. *Yield: Serves 4-6*

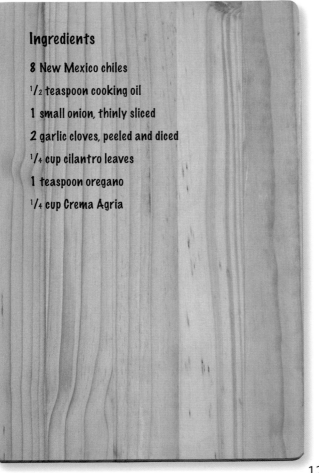

Ingredients

8 New Mexico chiles

1/2 teaspoon cooking oil

1 small onion, thinly sliced

2 garlic cloves, peeled and diced

1/4 cup cilantro leaves

1 teaspoon oregano

1/4 cup Crema Agria

Rajas con Crema

- Roast the chiles over an open flame or under a broiler until the skins are charred. Peel them, remove the seeds, and cut them into strips; set aside.

- Heat the oil in a large saucepan and sauté the onion 10 minutes.

- Add the garlic, cilantro, and oregano and sauté 3 more minutes.

- Remove from heat and stir in the Crema Agria to coat the vegetables.

• • • • RECIPE VARIATIONS • • • •

Rajas with Cheese: If you make Rajas con Crema as a side dish, you can add cheese, which makes it a little more rich and satisfying. Sprinkle a cup or so of shredded Queso Quesadilla over the top after stirring in the cream. To help melt the cheese, cover the pan. When the cheese has melted, serve immediately.

Rajas with Red Bell Pepper: For a more colorful version, substitute one poblano chile with a red bell pepper. Roast the pepper and peel it like you do the poblano and use as directed in the recipe. The addition of the pepper adds a subtle sweetness, so you can eliminate the cream.

Preparing the Chiles

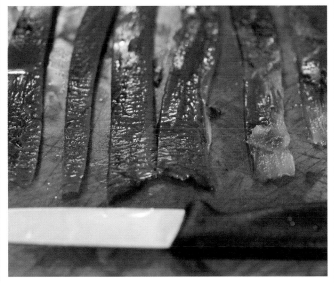

- After roasting the chiles until they blacken and blister, let them cool in an airtight container.

- When they are cool enough to touch, peel the charred skin off of each chile.

- Cut the stem off of each chile and then cut each chile in half and scrape out the seeds.

- Lay the chile halves flat on a cutting board and use a sharp knife to slice them lengthwise into ½-inch strips.

Cooking the Rajas

- Since the chiles were cooked during the roasting process they will not need much cooking.

- Sauté the onion until it begins to soften and becomes translucent.

- Sprinkle the seasonings evenly over the onion and chiles so they don't clump up in one area.

- Serve Rajas con Crema with a stack of warm flour or corn tortillas and additional onions and cilantro as garnishes.

ENSALADA FRESCA

This fresh green salad is garnished with avocado and seasoned with an abundance of Mexican flavor

When you think of Mexican food, you are probably drawn toward visions of tacos, stuffed chiles, and refried beans—not a crisp green salad. But when you visit local markets in Mexico, there is an abundance of fresh produce just ready to be crafted into a delicious ensalada fresca or fresh salad.

Most lettuce and tomatoes are used as toppings or garnishes for dishes like enchiladas or tostadas. They are eaten as part of the meal and would not necessarily be served on their own. With many new influences on Mexican cuisine in the recent years, the green salad is growing more popular. *Yield: Serves 2*

Ingredients

2 plum tomatoes

1/2 cup frozen corn

4 cups chopped romaine lettuce

1 cup cooked black beans

1/2 small red onion

Ensalada Fresca Dressing

1/4 cup cilantro leaves

1/2 cup tortilla chips, crushed

1/2 avocado, cut into 6 slices

Ensalada Fresca

- Chop the tomatoes and discard the excess seeds.

- Place the frozen corn in warm water to thaw and then drain when it has defrosted.

- In a large bowl, combine the lettuce, beans, tomatoes, onion, and corn; toss with Ensalada Fresca Dressing.

- Divide salad into 2 large serving bowls.

- Top each salad with cilantro leaves, crushed tortilla chips, and 3 avocado slices.

• • • • RECIPE VARIATION • • • •

Ensalada Fresca Dressing: In a blender combine 2 tablespoons lemon juice; 1 tablespoon white vinegar; $^1/_4$ cup olive oil; 3 garlic cloves; 1 teaspoon hot chile sauce; $^1/_4$ white onion, chopped; $^1/_4$ cup cilantro leaves; a pinch dry mustard; a pinch cumin; and $^1/_2$ teaspoon salt (or more to taste). Blend until smooth. Store dressing in an airtight container and refrigerate overnight for best flavor.

Selecting the Produce

- Use the freshest produce for the most delicious salad.

- For the best flavor, tomatoes should be fresh off the vine or have the vine still attached.

- Onions should have intact skins and no mold near the stem or root areas.

- Cilantro should look bright green and fresh without any brown spots.

- You can find locally grown, fresh produce at your local farmers' market.

Assembling the Salad

- Make sure the beans are rinsed and drained before adding them to the lettuce.

- Pour the dressing over all the ingredients and use tongs or 2 large forks to scoop the mixture around the bowl to combine the ingredients.

- The heavier ingredients such as the beans and tomatoes have a tendency to fall to the bottom. Make sure to scoop them back up to ensure the ingredients are evenly spread throughout the salad.

RED CHILE & CHEESE ENCHILADAS

Traditional cheese enchiladas taste great cooked in a zesty red chile sauce

Enchiladas can be found in various flavors and forms all over Mexico. Even street vendors serve up enchiladas smothered in sauce and topped with cheese. In its simplest form, an enchilada is merely a fresh corn tortilla dipped in warm chile sauce, folded, and eaten. Cheese and other fillings were later additions to this humble street food, and now there are as many versions of enchiladas as there are chefs.

While enchiladas are frequently made one at a time on a hot comal, you can also make them all at once, using the oven to heat them through and melt the cheese. The oven method also allows you to make enchiladas the night before and heat them when you are ready. *Yield: Serves 4–6*

Red Chile and Cheese Enchiladas

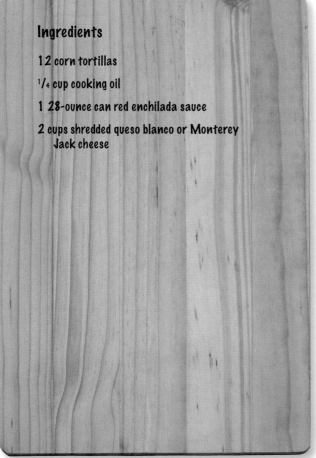

Ingredients

12 corn tortillas

¼ cup cooking oil

1 28-ounce can red enchilada sauce

2 cups shredded queso blanco or Monterey Jack cheese

- Lightly coat one of the tortillas with oil and heat on a warm comal.

- Dip the tortilla in a bowl of chile sauce until coated on both sides.

- Lay the tortilla in the bottom of a baking dish coated with cooking spray and place a couple of spoonfuls of cheese down the center.

- Roll up the tortilla and place it seam side down in the dish; repeat with remaining tortillas, sauce, and cheese. Top with remaining sauce and cheese.

- Bake 30 minutes at 350°F.

• • • • RECIPE VARIATION • • • •

Beef and Cheese Enchiladas: This is a great way to use leftover shredded beef from the night before. You need about 1 pound shredded beef and only half the cheese. Divide the beef evenly among the tortillas and top with just a sprinkle of cheese. Follow the recipe as directed.

MAKE IT EASY

You can assemble the enchiladas the night before and store them in the refrigerator until you are ready to bake them. Cover with plastic wrap so they don't dry out. Alternatively, you can make extra and freeze them for a quick meal at a later date. To heat frozen enchiladas, bake them uncovered 1 hour at 350°F.

Preparing the Tortillas

- Oiling and briefly cooking the tortillas help make them pliable so they are easy to roll.

- Each tortilla needs a very thin coating of oil. Too much oil will make the enchiladas greasy.

- When you place the tortilla on the warm comal, it is just to warm it; you don't want to overcook it or the tortilla will become crisp.

- You can pat the tortilla with a paper towel to absorb excess oil.

Preparing the Enchiladas

- Pour the chile sauce in a wide, shallow bowl or a 9x9 inch baking dish to allow for easier dipping.

- Chile sauce stains very easily, so wear an apron to protect your clothes and wipe up any drips immediately.

- Do not overstuff the tortillas. You will need just enough cheese so that the edges of the tortilla overlap by at least half of an inch when rolled over it.

ENSALADA NOPALITOS

This elegant arranged salad features tangy cactus and fresh tomatoes

Nopalitos are the pads of the prickly pear cactus that have been prepared for eating. The prickly pear is a native cactus and was eaten as food by the native peoples in the arid, dry climates of central Mexico, where the prickly pear cactus grew in abundance. Cactus is high in fiber and contains vitamin C. It is low in carbohydrates and helps promote healthy blood sugar.

You can buy fresh cactus pads and prepare them yourself by removing the spines, cutting them into pieces, and then boiling them—but canned cactus is a fine replacement.

This salad is a typical ensalada nopalitos, which is arranged on a platter rather than tossed together like most salads. *Yield: Serves 4–6*

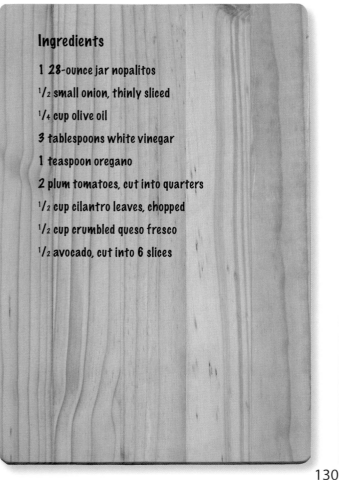

Ingredients

1 28-ounce jar nopalitos

1/2 small onion, thinly sliced

1/4 cup olive oil

3 tablespoons white vinegar

1 teaspoon oregano

2 plum tomatoes, cut into quarters

1/2 cup cilantro leaves, chopped

1/2 cup crumbled queso fresco

1/2 avocado, cut into 6 slices

Ensalada Nopalitos

- Drain the liquid from the nopalitos, rinse them thoroughly, and drain again. Place them in a mixing bowl with the onion.

- Whisk together the olive oil, vinegar, and oregano and pour over the nopalitos and onion. Let the mixture marinate in the refrigerator 30 minutes.

- Add the tomatoes to the mixture and toss to coat.

- Spread the nopalitos mixture on a platter and top with cilantro, cheese, and avocado slices.

•••• RECIPE VARIATION ••••

Grilled Ensalada Nopalitos: Remove the spines from the pad with a paring knife and grill it over direct heat until it begins to brown and soften. Cut it into cubes and marinate in ¼ cup lemon juice, 2 tablespoons oil, and a pinch salt for at least 30 minutes. Refrigerate until ready to use.

ZOOM

Because the cactus is from a jar, make sure the rest of your produce is farm fresh so as to bring those refreshing flavors to the salad. This salad is especially delicious with fresh-picked tomatoes.

Marinating the Nopalitos

- The nopalitos need time to absorb the flavors from the oil and vinegar. Thirty minutes should be sufficient, but you can marinate them overnight in the refrigerator if necessary.

- Do not add the tomatoes until you are ready to serve the salad; the marinade could make them mushy.

- After you toss the nopalitos in the marinade, cover it and place in the refrigerator until ready to use.

Plating the Ensalada Nopalitos

- When preparing Ensalada Nopalitos, the presentation is very important.

- Spread the nopalitos evenly across the bottom of a platter.

- Add the onions and tomatoes evenly over the nopalitos, making sure they are evenly distributed.

- If some ingredients fall to the bottom, pull them to the top so you can see an equal amount of everything.

FLOUR TORTILLAS

Tender and chewy, use this bread to hold fillings or serve it alongside a main dish

Flour tortillas are the mainstay of the northern Mexican diet, much like sandwich bread is in the United States. They are stuffed with fillings to make tacos or burritos, they are used to sop up the last drops of soup from a nearly empty bowl, or they are rolled up and eaten fresh off the comal. The aroma of fresh tortillas is enough to make your mouth water; you'll be counting the seconds until they have cooled enough for you to take a bite.

Flour tortillas have been gradually gaining popularity outside of Mexico and are now consumed more than bagels.

Once they're made fresh in your own kitchen, you won't ever want to use store-bought tortillas again. *Yield: 12 Tortillas*

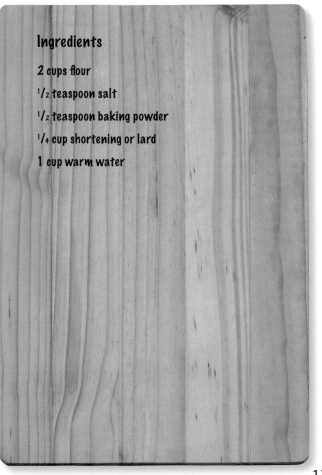

Ingredients

2 cups flour

1/2 teaspoon salt

1/2 teaspoon baking powder

1/4 cup shortening or lard

1 cup warm water

Flour Tortillas

- Place the flour in a mixing bowl. Sprinkle the salt and baking powder over the flour.

- Add the shortening in 4 or 5 small chunks. Blend the shortening into the flour with a pastry blender.

- Add water until a soft dough forms. Knead 5 minutes and separate into 12 portions.

- Roll out each portion into a tortilla that is about 6 inches across. Cook it on a medium-hot comal about 1 minute on each side.

• • • • RECIPE VARIATIONS • • • •

Roasted Garlic Tortillas: Experiment with added flavorings and seasonings to create new and unique tortillas. Roast a head of garlic in a 300°F oven until soft. Squeeze the garlic into the tortilla dough with an extra pinch of salt and a few tablespoons of chopped parsley.

Reheating the Tortillas: Tortillas begin to lose their moisture as soon as they begin to cool, and by the following day they may become stiff and dry. You can quickly reheat them by warming them one at time on a hot comal, or you can steam them by wrapping a stack in a damp towel and heating them in a microwave 1 to 2 minutes.

Rolling the Tortilla

- Roll each dough portion into a round ball and then flatten it between your palms.

- Roll the dough 2 or 3 times into an oval shape. Then turn the dough one quarter turn and roll again.

- Continue to turn the dough one quarter until you have made an even circle.

- The dough should not stick because of the lard, so you do not need to flour the dough or work surface.

Cooking the Tortilla

- Heat the comal over medium-high heat and adjust as necessary to maintain a consistent heat level.

- While the tortilla is cooking, it may puff up. It will deflate as soon as you remove it from the comal. Lightly press it down if you feel the tortilla is not cooking evenly.

- Tortillas are ready after about a minute, when they start to develop brown spots. Flip it over and cook the other side.

- Keep tortillas wrapped in a towel to keep them warm.

CORN TORTILLAS

These little disks of masa have long been the cornerstone of the Mexican diet

Corn tortillas have been the foundation of the Mexican diet since the ancient days of the Mayans and Aztecs. Corn kernels were treated with wood ash to help remove the hulls. The resulting soft corn was ground into dough and then flattened into tortillas by hand. The tortillas were often used to scoop up food or wrapped around a filling similar to a taco.

Today people use corn tortillas in much the same way the native Mexicans did thousands of years ago. Fillings are piled on, creating a taco, or they are served with main dishes to be eaten as part of the meal. Corn tortillas can also be cut up and fried into crunchy chips, which make a delicious snack or appetizer. *Yield: 12 Tortillas*

Ingredients

2 cups masa harina

1 1/2 cups warm water

Corn Tortillas

- Place masa harina in a mixing bowl and add the water.

- Use your hands to form a dough and knead 2 minutes.

- Divide the dough into 12 portions; roll each into a ball and press each on a tortilla press.

- As you press each tortilla, cook it on a comal heated over medium-high heat and cook 45 seconds on each side.

MAKE IT EASY

Fresh masa can be found in Mexican markets and is an ideal choice for corn tortillas. It is ready to go and needs no added water. Form the dough into balls and follow the recipe to form the tortillas with the press and cook them on a comal.

···· YELLOW ● LIGHT ····

Masa harina is "masa flour," meaning it is masa that has been dried and then ground into a flour. Do not attempt to substitute cornmeal or corn flour for the masa, as they are processed much differently. Using cornmeal or corn flour will not result in a traditional tortilla.

Pressing the Tortillas

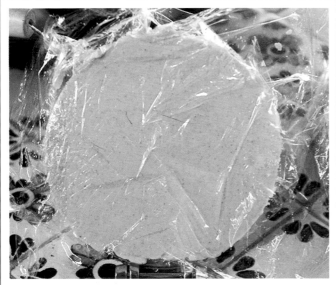

Cooking the Tortillas

- You want the dough to be pliable. If it is too stiff, add more water by the teaspoon until it is softened. If the dough is sticking to your fingers, add more masa harina by the tablespoon until it stops sticking.

- Cover each side of the press with plastic wrap and press a ball of dough into a tortilla.

- If you don't have a press, roll out the dough between two pieces of plastic wrap; it most likely will not make a perfect circle.

- Heat the comal over medium-high heat 1 or 2 minutes or until hot.

- Cook each tortilla as it comes off the press, otherwise it will stick to just about anything you set it on.

- The tortillas will puff up with steam but will flatten back out when removed from the heat.

- Keep the fresh tortillas wrapped in a towel to keep them warm while you cook the rest.

BOLILLOS

This crusty roll is a staple in Mexico and baked fresh daily in local panaderias

Bolillos are very similar in texture to French bread. They are golden and crusty on the outside, soft and chewy on the inside. They are used for making tortas, a Mexican sandwich, and are utilized anywhere that plain white bread is called for. Other shapes are available, but bolillos are the most popular bread for everyday consumption.

Panaderias, or Mexican bakeries, make up batches of freshly made bolillos every day. They contain no preservatives and must be consumed within a couple of days, so most families buy fresh bread 3 or 4 times a week. *Yield: 10 Bolillos*

Ingredients

1 1/2 cups warm water

2 teaspoons dry yeast

3 cups flour

1 1/2 tablespoons sugar

1 1/2 teaspoons salt

Bolillos

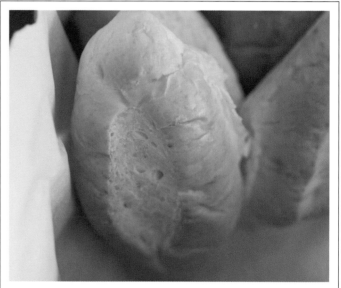

- Pour the warm water into a bowl and sprinkle the yeast over it. In a separate bowl, combine remaining ingredients.

- Add the water mixure to the flour mixture and combine until a dough forms. Place dough in a greased bowl, cover, and let sit 1 hour.

- Remove dough from bowl and knead 10 minutes. Divide dough into 10 equal portions and shape each into a bolillo. Cover and let rise 30 minutes.

- Score each roll down the center twice; bake 20 minutes at 375°F.

136

Using a Bread Maker: If you have a bread maker, you can use it to prepare the dough for bolillos. Place all the ingredients into the bread maker according to the manufacturer's instructions and set it to the dough cycle. When the dough is ready, form the bolillos by hand and bake as directed.

Tortas: Bolillos are cut in half and filled with ingredients to make a torta, or Mexican sandwich. To make a torta, spread half of a bolillo with beans. Top it with shredded chicken, shredded lettuce, sliced tomatoes, pickled jalapeños, and sliced avocado or guacamole. Place the other half of the bolillo on top and you've got yourself a delicious torta.

Preparing the Dough

- The water should be slightly warmer than room temperature.

- Sift the flour, sugar, and salt together to make sure they are evenly combined.

- While dough is rising, keep it in a warm area of your kitchen.

- Keep the bowl with the dough covered with a slightly damp cloth so the surface does not dry out.

Forming the Bolillos

- Roll the dough into a ball first. Then roll it on a flat surface with your palm until the ends begin to get pointy.

- Move your hand to one end and roll it more to emphasize the point; repeat on the other side.

- Using a knife, make 1 long score lengthwise down each bolillo.

- Place the rolls on a lightly greased baking sheet and bake until golden brown.

ROSCA DE REYES

Enjoy this slightly sweet bread topped with candied fruit over the winter holidays

Rosca de Reyes or Three Kings Cake is a type of bread enjoyed on and around January 6 to celebrate the Epiphany. A little doll is baked inside the bread to represent the baby Jesus. Tradition says that whoever finds the doll within his or her piece of bread is supposed to provide the tamales for the next holiday celebration.

The bread is a prepared with a rich dough made of eggs, butter, and sugar. The dough is formed into a round or oval wreath and then toppings are added. The toppings consist of sweet candied fruits and strips of a sweet crumb topping. The final bread is slightly sweet and infused with anise and other spices. *Yield: Serves 8–10*

Ingredients

¹/₃ cup warm water

1 packet yeast

4 cups flour

1 cup sugar

¹/₂ teaspoon salt

1 teaspoon cinnamon

¹/₂ teaspoon anise seed

4 extra-large eggs, beaten

¹/₂ cup orange juice

³/₄ cup butter, softened

3 teaspoons vanilla

Crumb Topping

2 cups assorted dried fruit strips

1 egg beaten

¹/₃ cup sugar

Rosca de Reyes

- Sprinkle the yeast onto the surface of the water; set aside.

- In a large bowl sift together the dry ingredients; make a well in the center and add the yeast mixture and remaining ingredients (through the vanilla).

- Using your hands combine ingredients into a dough. Cover and let rise 2 hours.

- Form the dough into a wreath, decorate with Crumb Topping and dried fruit, and let rise until doubled. Brush with egg, sprinkle with sugar, and bake 45 minutes at 350°F.

• • • • RECIPE VARIATION • • • •

Crumb Topping: In a mixing bowl combine ¹/₄ cup shortening, ¹/₄ cup powdered sugar, ¹/₄ cup granulated sugar, ¹/₂ cup flour, 1 tablespoon water, and 1 teaspoon vanilla and mix on medium speed until a soft dough forms. Scrape the sides often to incorporate all ingredients. Roll dough into a ball and place on a lightly floured surface. Roll out into a square about five or six inches across and about ¹/₈-inch thick. Cut the dough into strips.

Shaping the Dough

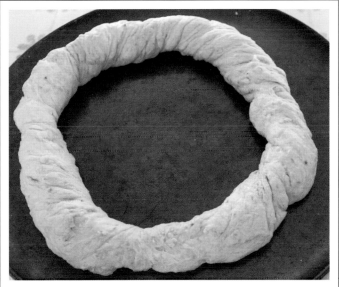

- After the dough has risen, punch it down and knead 2 minutes.

- Roll the dough into a log shape and bring the ends together to form a circle.

- Push the ends of the dough together and reshape with your fingers to make it smooth.

- The wreath will be around 12 inches in diameter.

Decorating the Dough

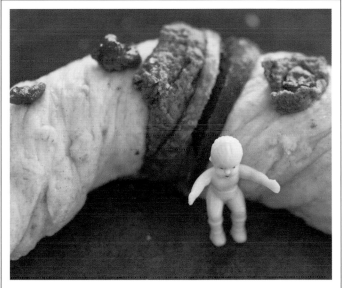

- After forming the wreath, let the dough rise until it has doubled in size.

- Press pieces of Crumb Topping across the top of the dough.

- Press the dried fruit into the top of the dough between the Crumb Topping.

- Lightly brush the wreath with the egg and sprinkle with sugar.

PAN DE MUERTO

The Day of the Dead festivities wouldn't be the same without this festive sweet bread

In Mexico there is a celebration for those who have passed on. The idea is that the spirits of the deceased return on the first and second days of November, and altars are made to honor them.

Food and drink as well as personal items are displayed on the altars to draw the spirits and help prepare them for the long journey. Pan de Muerto or Bread of the Dead is placed on the altars as well as consumed during the Dia de los Muertos or Day of the Dead festivities. Pan de Muerto is a slightly sweet loaf of bread that is a rounded mound shape and decorated with knobby forms that represent bones. After the bread is baked, it is glazed and topped with sugar. *Yield: Serves 6–8*

Ingredients

¹/₂ cup butter

³/₄ cup sugar

2 tablespoons orange zest

2 teaspoons whole anise seed

1 teaspoon salt

4 large eggs

2 packets dry yeast dissolved in 1¹/₄ cups warm water

6 cups flour

Glaze

¹/₂ cup sugar

Pan de Muerto

- Mix together the butter, sugar, zest, anise, and salt.

- In another bowl, mix together the eggs and yeast; combine with butter mixture. Add flour 1 cup at a time, mixing each time.

- Knead dough and let rise in a covered bowl for about an hour. Punch down the dough and pinch off one fourth. Form the dough into a large loaf; use the smaller piece of dough to make bone shapes.

- Bake 30 minutes at 350°F. Once cool, apply Glaze and sprinkle with sugar.

• • • • RECIPE VARIATIONS • • • •

Orange Glaze: Place ³/₄ cup granulated sugar and ¹/₂ cup orange juice into a small pot over low heat. Let it simmer until sugar dissolves. Cool slightly before using.

Cranberry Glaze: Place 4 ounces piloncillo, ¹/₄ cup granulated sugar, ²/₃ cup cranberry juice, and 1 tablespoon orange zest into a small pot over low heat. Let it simmer until sugar dissolves. Cool slightly before using.

Creating the Pan de Muerto

- The loaf portion of the bread is round and slightly flattened.

- With the smaller portion of the dough, roll out long pieces with knobs on the ends. Place one flattened ball of dough in the center.

- Add the bone shapes before the dough rises the last time.

- The "bones" should stem from the center ball and radiate toward the edge.

Decorating the Pan de Muerto

- Let the bread cool completely before adding the Glaze.

- Lightly brush on a thin coat of Glaze over the entire loaf. If you still have a lot of Glaze left, let it partially dry on the loaf and then layer on another coat.

- Sprinkle sugar over the glaze and let the glaze dry.

- Work in sections if the glaze dries or absorbs into the bread too quickly.

PAN DULCE

This subtly sweet bread is topped with colorful toppings carved into decorative designs

Pan dulce, or sweet bread, is a staple for breakfast and snacks alike. The bread is baked daily in Mexican bakeries called panaderias and is particularly good with a hot cup of coffee. The bread is soft and chewy, and the sugary topping is cut into designs, which the bread is named for. Pan dulce is also known as conchas, which are named for the topping's shell shape.

Fresh Mexican bread is made with very few preservatives, so pan dulce must be consumed within a day or two, which is generally not a problem. Try this delicious bread with your next cup of morning coffee. *Yield: Makes 16 Pan Dulces*

Ingredients

2 tablespoons vegetable shortening

$^1/_3$ cup sugar

4 extra-large eggs, beaten and at room temperature

1 teaspoon salt

1 package dry yeast mixed into $^1/_2$ cup lukewarm water

$3^1/_2$ cups flour

Crumb Topping

Pan Dulce

- In a large bowl, cream the shortening and sugar. Slowly add in eggs, salt, and the water with the yeast.

- Add 1 cup flour at a time until incorporated. Knead dough 3 minutes, cover, and let rise in a warm place 45 minutes.

- Divide dough into 16 balls. Place on a lightly greased baking sheet and slightly press each ball to flatten it.

- Place Crumb Topping on dough, cover, and let rise 1 hour. Bake 15 minutes at 350°F.

• • • • RECIPE VARIATION • • • •

Crumb Topping: Mix ¹/₂ cup shortening, ¹/₂ cup powdered sugar, ¹/₂ cup granulated sugar, 1 cup flour, 3 teaspoons vanilla, 1 teaspoon water, and food coloring, if desired, in a mixer on medium speed until a dough forms. It should be slightly stiffer than cookie dough. Make this topping up to 24 hours in advance and store it in the refrigerator. Bring it to room temperature before using.

Adding the Crumb Topping

- Divide the Crumb Topping into 16 equal portions and roll each into a ball.

- Flatten each ball between the palms of your hands until it is just large enough to cover the dough and is about ⅛-inch thick.

- Place topping onto the dough and lightly press down so it adheres.

- If the topping gets warm, it may become greasy, so do this step in a cool area.

Creating Designs

- Carefully drag a sharp, straight-edged knife through the topping to make designs.

- Create the designs in small and tight dimensions, as the bread and topping will expand during baking.

- Cut deeply enough to slice through the topping, but not into the bread dough.

- If you do not carve a specific design, the topping will crack during baking, creating its own unique design.

RED CHILE SALSA

This salsa features guajillo chiles, which provide medium heat and a delicious earthy flavor

Guajillo chiles are very popular in Mexico and are a major part of the chile-farming industry. They are usually found as dried pods that can be ground into guaillo chile powder or made into a chile paste. They have a reddish brown color and are well suited to almost any recipe that calls for dried chiles.

Guajillos benefit from being toasted on a hot comal before soaking them. They require a long soaking time because they are tough and leathery. Guajillos are a great ingredient for salsa because they have a lot of rich, smoky flavor and they are not overly spicy. *Yield: Serves 4–6*

Ingredients

3 beefsteak tomatoes

$1/2$ onion, peeled

4 dried guajillo chiles

1 red bell pepper

1 cup cilantro leaves

4 garlic cloves, peeled

2 tablespoons oil

2 limes, juiced

1 tablespoon vinegar

1 teaspoon salt

Red Chile Salsa

- Coarsely chop the tomatoes, discarding the watery seed portion, and cut the onion into large chunks.

- Toast and rehydrate the guajillo chiles and cut into chunks.

- Cut the stem off the bell pepper, remove the seeds, and cut into chunks.

- Add all ingredients to a food processor and process a few seconds at a time until the ingredients are well combined.

Guajillos are a great choice for this salsa because they have a rich, earthy flavor but are not overpowering. If guajillos are not available, there are other chiles that also make great salsa. Pasilla chiles are a bit more spicy and have a unique herb flavor. Other delicious chiles are the Anaheim and New Mexico chiles, which are milder than the guajillo but still delicious.

How to Select Guajillo Chiles: Look for dried chiles that have a uniform dark reddish brown color. The chiles should be intact without any tears or holes. Avoid chiles with any light spots, as they may indicate mold or fungus. Dried guajillos should be tough and pliable, not brittle.

Toasting the Chiles

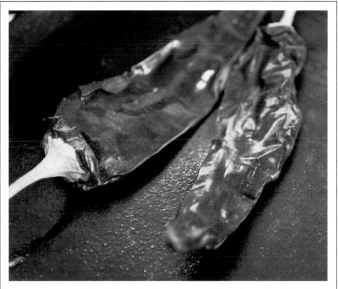

- Heat a comal slowly to high heat.

- Place the dried chiles on the hot comal and toast about 30 seconds on each side until browned and fragrant.

- Soak the toasted chiles in warm water 30 minutes or until softened.

- Cut the stems off the chiles and use a spoon to scrape out the seeds.

Making the Salsa

- Make sure the ingredients are chopped into pieces of similar size.

- Place all the ingredients in the food processor at one time so they blend evenly.

- This salsa is supposed to have some texture, so don't overprocess and make it smooth.

- If the salsa seems too thick, you can add some of the chile soaking liquid to thin it out.

SALSA VERDE

This tangy green salsa gets its signature flavor from roasted green chiles and fresh tomatillos

Salsa verde, or green salsa, is different from green chile sauce because it contains tomatillos, which give the salsa its signature flavor. It can be served warm as in a stew type dish or lightly chilled or at room temperature as a condiment or topping.

Tomatillos are a native Mexican ingredient and are widely available outside of Mexico. They have a light green, papery husk that hovers around the tomatillo without actually touching it. The husk is removed to reveal a sticky bright green fruit that is tart and flavorful. Tomatillos range in size from a small walnut to a golf ball. If you can get a hold of some fresh tomatillos, you have got to try this delicious salsa.

Yield: Serves 4–6

Ingredients

12 tomatillos

4 Anaheim chiles

1 medium white onion

1 bunch cilantro

5 cloves garlic

1 teaspoon vegetable oil

1 tablespoon lime juice

Salt to taste

1/2 cup water, as needed

Salsa Verde

- Remove the husks from the tomatillos, rinse them thoroughly to remove the sticky residue, and then cut them into quarters.

- Char the Anaheim chiles and remove the skins, seeds, and stems.

- Coarsely chop the onion and cilantro.

- Add all the ingredients except the water to a food processor and mix on low speed until ingredients are combined.

Salsa Verde with Avocado: Cut an avocado in half and remove the seed. Use a spoon to scoop out the flesh and cut it into large chunks. Add with the avocado to the rest of the ingredients. Adjust the amount of avocado according to your taste.

Salsa Verde with Roasted Tomatillos: Remove the husks from the tomatillos and rinse them well to remove the sticky residue. Leave them whole and place them on a hot grill or under a broiler until they begin to soften and brown. Let them cool completely before cutting them into chunks and blending with the salsa.

Preparing the Chiles

- Char the green chiles under a broiler, on a grill, or on a hot comal.

- The chile is ready when the skin is blackened and blistered.

- Place the chiles in an airtight container 2 minutes to let the steam help loosen the skins.

- The skin should come off easily; run it under water to help loosen any stubborn pieces.

Processing the Salsa

- Salt is the key to the flavor of this tangy salsa, so add plenty of it to taste.

- Make sure all the ingredients are cut into manageable pieces before processing.

- The mixture should not be thick. If it is too thick, add the water a little at a time, processing after each addition, until a thinner consistency is achieved. It should be about as thin as tomato sauce.

SALSAS

ROASTED CHILE SALSA
Roasting the chiles, tomatoes, and onions gives this salsa its rich smoky flavor

Modern recipes for salsas include two main ingredients: tomatoes and chiles. Similar combinations of tomatoes and chiles can be traced back to the Aztecs. Chiles are native to Mexico, and tomatoes made their way north into Mexico from South America.

The ingredients for salsa can be raw or cooked or a combination of both. The ingredients can be pureed together or chopped separately and then tossed together. One way to extract flavor from a tomato or chile is to roast it. The ingredients in Roasted Chile Salsa are roasted to bring out their subtle flavors and add new layers of taste and aroma. *Yield: Serves 4–6*

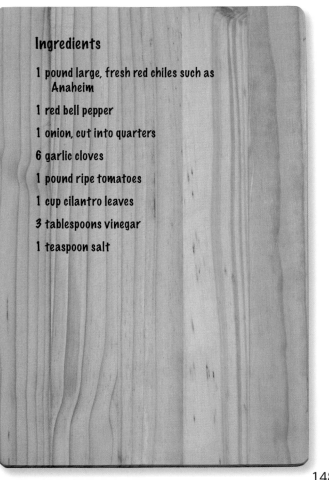

Ingredients

1 pound large, fresh red chiles such as Anaheim

1 red bell pepper

1 onion, cut into quarters

6 garlic cloves

1 pound ripe tomatoes

1 cup cilantro leaves

3 tablespoons vinegar

1 teaspoon salt

Roasted Chile Salsa

- Roast the chiles and bell pepper until the skins are blackened. Peel the skins off and remove the stems and seeds.

- Place the onion quarters, garlic, and tomatoes onto a baking sheet and brown them under a broiler.

- Let the tomatoes cool, cut the stem area out, and use a spoon to scoop out the majority of the seeds and liquid.

- Place all the ingredients into a food processor and process until combined.

• • • • RECIPE VARIATION • • • •

Selecting Red Chiles: Your local farmers' market or Latin market is probably the best place to find fresh chiles. Look for chiles that are bright and uniform in color with smooth and shiny skin. They should smell fresh and not have any mold or mildew around the stem. Do not purchase chiles with dark spots; they could be infected with fungus.

ZOOM

If fresh red chiles are not available, substitute fresh green chiles such as New Mexico or poblano chiles. The green chiles will give the salsa a more muted neutral color rather than a bright red tone, but it will still have excellent flavor.

SALSAS

Roasting the Vegetables

- The chiles need blackened skins to make them easy to peel.

- The onion needs to be quartered so that there is a maximum amount of surface area that can brown and add flavor.

- The tomatoes need to remain whole while roasting so the juices don't make a mess.

- Peel the garlic cloves before roasting them.

Finishing the Salsa

- The salsa should have some texture; it should not be completely smooth.

- You can enjoy the salsa immediately, or let it rest in the refrigerator overnight so the flavors can blend.

- Serve the salsa with your favorite tortilla chips or use it as topping for tacos or as a sauce for burritos.

BEAN & CORN SALSA

Beans and corn are native Mexican ingredients that blend together beautifully in this salsa

Beans and corn are native Mexican ingredients used thousands of years ago as staples for the Mayan and Aztec diets. Aztecs also used salsas as sauces or condiments to other dishes, and these salsas always included tomatoes and chiles.

Bean and Corn Salsa combines the earthy flavors of black beans with the fresh, sweet flavors of corn. The usual salsa components of tomatoes and chiles round out the flavors and prove a traditional backdrop for this sweet and savory salsa.

This salsa is delicious when eaten with tortilla chips, and the sweet fruity flavors are a great companion for chicken and fish dishes. *Yield: Serves 6–8*

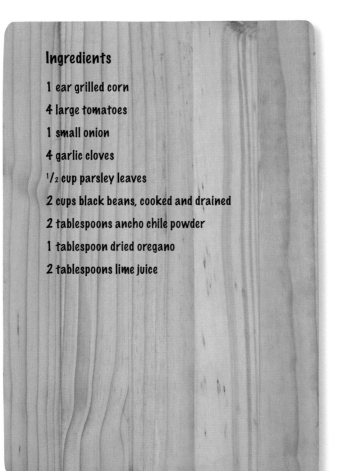

Ingredients

1 ear grilled corn

4 large tomatoes

1 small onion

4 garlic cloves

1/2 cup parsley leaves

2 cups black beans, cooked and drained

2 tablespoons ancho chile powder

1 tablespoon dried oregano

2 tablespoons lime juice

Bean and Corn Salsa

- Slice the corn off the cob.

- Dice the tomatoes into ¼-inch pieces, discarding the seeds and liquid.

- Peel the onion and dice it into ¼-pieces.

- Peel the garlic cloves and chop them into fine pieces.

- Coarsely chop the parsley until it is about half the volume.

- Combine all of the ingredients in a large bowl and toss to combine.

150

Using Frozen or Canned Corn: For a quick and easy salsa, substitute the fresh grilled corn for frozen or canned corn that has been rinsed and drained. To get the roasted flavor of grilling, cook the corn in 1 teaspoon oil in a hot pan, just until the kernels begin to brown. Let the corn cool completely before adding it to the salsa.

Using Canned Tomatoes: If you don't have any fresh tomatoes, use canned tomatoes. Some canned tomatoes have added seasonings, so be sure to use the plain variety. Drain the liquid off and chop the tomatoes into $\frac{1}{2}$-inch pieces. Heat 1 teaspoon oil in a saucepan over medium heat and cook the tomatoes 2 minutes, stirring frequently, to help soften the flavor. Let them cool completely before adding them.

Grilling the Corn

- Remove the husk and strings off of the corn and brush it with a light coat of oil; sprinkle with salt and pepper.

- Heat a grill over medium-high heat and cook the corn about 5 minutes, turning it frequently. You can also cook the corn in a 450°F oven 5 to 10 minutes.

- You can grill the corn up to 1 day in advance and store it in the refrigerator until ready to use.

- Use a sharp knife to cut the kernels of corn off before adding it the bowl.

Preparing the Tomatoes

- Use a very sharp knife to cut the tomatoes. If the knife pushes on the tomato before it cuts it, it is too dull.

- Cut the flesh away from the seeds in large chunks. Discard the seeds and liquid.

- Lay the tomato pieces and press them slightly to flatten them.

- Cut each piece into strips and then cut the strips across to create ¼-inch pieces.

SALSAS

MANGO SALSA

The tropical flavors of Mexico are unleashed in this deliciously fruity salsa

During mango season in Mexico, street vendors sell mangos that are carved into flower-like designs, served on sticks like a Popsicle, and enjoyed by adults and children alike. Chile flavors go well with this sweet fruit, and chile powder is often sprinkled on the carved mangos.

Mangos are a tropical fruit, and Mexico is one of the largest exporters of this delicious produce.

In this salsa the fresh, tropical flavors of mango are paired with luscious ripe tomatoes and spicy jalapeños. The combination of sweet and spicy is typical of Mexican cuisine, and the contrasting flavor combinations are found in many Mexican dishes. *Yield: Serves 4–6*

Ingredients

3 plum tomatoes

2 mangos

1 jalapeño

1/2 small red onion

1 garlic clove

1/2 cup cilantro leaves

1/2 teaspoon of salt

1/2 teaspoon ground white pepper

1 tablespoon lemon juice

1 tablespoon olive oil

Mango Salsa

- Chop the tomatoes and discard the seeds.

- Cut the mango off the seed and away from the skin in small chunks.

- Cut the stem off the jalapeño and remove the seeds; finely dice.

- Chop the onion, garlic, and cilantro.

- Place all the ingredients in a large bowl and toss until combined.

Selecting a Mango: A ripe mango should give just slightly when lightly squeezed. Avoid unripe mangos because they often become mushy before they ripen. The color gives very little indication as to whether a mango is ripe or not, so don't be afraid of a green one if it gives slightly to the touch. Black spots can indicate ripeness, but avoid overripe, soft, or mushy mangos.

Pineapple and Peach Salsa: Tart pineapples and sweet peaches make a delicious combination if mangoes are unavailable. Remove the skin from the pineapple and cut the flesh off the core. You need 1 cup pineapple cut into $1/2$-inch pieces. Remove the pit from the peach and peel the skin off. You need $1/2$ cup peach cut into $1/2$-inch pieces. Use the pineapple and peach in place of the mango.

Preparing the Mango

- Slice each half of the mango off of the wide flat seed that lies in the center.

- Score each mango half lengthwise and then crosswise. Your knife should cut through the flesh but not through the skin.

- Hold the mango half in both hands and use your thumbs to press on the center.

- Slice the cubes of mango off the skin with a sharp knife.

Finishing the Mango Salsa

- Ripe mangos are usually pretty soft in texture, so fold the ingredients together carefully so the mangos don't become mushy.

- Make sure all the ingredients are cut to a uniform

- size, except for the onions and garlic, which should be finely diced.

- Place the salsa in an airtight container and refrigerate overnight to allow the flavors to fully incorporate.

SALSAS

HABAÑERO SALSA

This insanely spicy salsa is delicious with chips or as a topping for fish or chicken

The habañero chile is one of the spiciest in the world. It typically has a bright orange color, but can sometimes have a red or yellow hue. Habañero chiles originated in the Yucatan Peninsula region of Mexico thousands of years ago and are still widely used to season and flavor a variety of dishes. When the Europeans discovered the spicy chile, they brought it back to their homelands and its popularity quickly spread beyond Europe and into Asia.

If you can get past the fiery heat the habañero provides, you can begin to enjoy the subtle fruity flavors. Because of their fruit flavors, habañeros are delicious in salsas. *Yield: Serves 6–8*

Ingredients

4 large tomatoes

2 habañero chiles

2 jalapeño chiles

1 small red onion

3 garlic cloves

2 tablespoons lemon juice

1/2 teaspoon salt

Habañero Salsa

- Seed and dice the tomatoes, discarding most of the seeds and pulp, and place them in a large bowl.

- Roast chiles on a hot comal, cut them in half, scrape out the seeds, and remove the stems.

- Finely chop the chiles and add them to the tomatoes.

- Dice the onion and garlic and add them to the mixture.

- Sprinkle the lemon juice and salt over the top and fold the mixture to thoroughly incorporate it.

•••• RECIPE VARIATIONS ••••

Scotch Bonnet Salsa: Scotch bonnets chiles are closely related to the habañero chile, so they make a wonderful replacement if habañeros are unavailable. Scotch bonnets are used widely in Caribbean and Jamaican cuisine and are just as hot and spicy as the habañero, but they have a slightly fruity flavor. Use two Scotch bonnets in place of the two habañeros.

Working with Hot Chiles: The capsaicin in chiles is what causes them to burn unprotected skin and eyes. The chemical is concentrated in the white veins and seeds, so to reduce the heat, remove these from the chiles. Wear gloves when handling habañeros and keep your hands away from your eyes and face while working with them.

Preparing the Habañeros

- Heat a comal over low heat and slowly turn it up to high heat.

- Cook the habañeros and jalapeños on the hot comal until the skins begin to brown and blister on each side.

- Wearing gloves, carefully cut each habañero and jalapeño in half. Carefully scrape out the seeds with a spoon.

- Use a sharp knife to cut off the stems, being careful of any juices that might squirt out.

Preparing the Salsa

- Let the habañeros and jalapeños cool completely before adding them to the other ingredients.

- Let the salsa rest in the refrigerator overnight so the flavors can fully blend.

- Let the salsa return to room temperature before serving to allow the flavors to fully unfold.

- Make sure to warn guests about the heat level of the salsa, as it may be overwhelming for some.

CHICKEN SOFT TACOS

These scrumptious soft tacos are filled with juicy chicken cooked with onions and tomatoes

Flour tortillas are a mainstay of the northern Mexican diet and are often stuffed with fillings and enjoyed as tacos. Because flour tortillas have a soft and chewy texture, tacos that use flour tortillas have been dubbed "soft tacos."

Soft tacos are in contrast to another popular north-of-the-border taco shell made with processed corn formed into a U shape and fried until crunchy.

Flour tortillas are mild in flavor and pair well with the subtle taste of chicken breast. Garlic and onion add additional flavors, and ground cumin and chile lend a smokiness that goes well with the native staples of tomatoes and chiles. *Yield: Serves 6*

Ingredients

2 tablespoons cooking oil

2 boneless, skinless chicken breasts, pounded to $1/2$-inch thickness

1 small onion, chopped

3 garlic cloves, chopped

1 red bell pepper, stems and seeds removed and chopped

3 plum tomatoes, chopped

1 15-ounce can chicken broth

$1/2$ teaspoon cumin

1 teaspoon ground chile powder

12 flour tortillas

$1/2$ cup fresh salsa

$1/2$ cup crumbled queso fresco

Chicken Soft Tacos

- In a large saucepan heat the oil over medium heat. Add the chicken and cook 8 minutes on each side, until it is 170°F. Remove from pan; slice into strips.

- Add the onion, garlic, red pepper, and tomatoes to the hot pan; sauté over medium heat 2 minutes.

- Add the chicken, broth, and seasonings; cook over high heat until the liquid cooks off, about 15 minutes.

- Place equal portions of filling onto each flour tortilla and top with salsa and queso fresco.

MAKE IT AHEAD

You can make the chicken mixture up to 1 day in advance. Cook it as directed and then let it cool completely before covering and storing in the refrigerator. Simply reheat the mixture in a saucepan over low heat or in the microwave.

• • • • RECIPE VARIATION • • • •

Vegetarian Soft Tacos: Instead of the chicken, use 2 or 3 portabella mushroom caps. Brush on a light coat of oil and grill them a few minutes, until they begin to soften. Cut them into bite-size pieces. Also, use vegetable broth instead of chicken broth.

Cooking the Filling

- Sauté the vegetables until they begin to wilt and soften. Do not overcook or they will become mushy.

- Wait until the vegetables are done before adding the chicken to the pan;

it is already cooked and only needs to be warmed through.

- Add the broth slowly and carefully, as it may splatter when it comes in contact with the hot pan.

Heating the Tortillas

- Use a damp towel to help steam the tortillas. Place a stack of tortillas on the damp towel, wrap them up, and microwave them 1 minute or until heated through.

- You can also place the towel-wrapped tortillas in a

covered casserole dish and heat in a 300°F oven 10 to 15 minutes.

- Keep the tortillas in a tortilla warmer so they stay warm until used to make the tacos.

TACOS & TOSTADAS

CARNE ASADA TACOS

These delectable tacos are sold by Mexican street vendors as a snack food

Tacos in Mexico are like a sandwich in the United States. They can be filled with a variety of ingredients and are often sold by street vendors in the evening and through the early hours of the morning.

Carne asada tacos are one of the most popular versions, with juicy grilled steak topped with onions, cilantro, and chile sauce.

The fillings are served wrapped in a double layer of soft corn tortillas that are only about 5 inches in diameter. The tacos are often wrapped individually in foil wrappers, which help soften the tortilla, as the heat and moisture trapped inside create a steaming effect. *Yield: Serves 4*

Ingredients

¹/₂ cup chile sauce

2 limes, juiced

1 pound skirt steak

16 small corn tortillas

8 squares foil (9x9 inch or larger)

¹/₂ cup onion, diced

¹/₂ cup cilantro, chopped

Carne Asada Tacos

- Whisk together the chile sauce and lime juice and marinate the steak in the mixture 30 minutes.

- Grill the steak over medium-high heat until it is cooked through; let rest 5 minutes.

- Using a sharp knife cut the meat against the grain into bite-size pieces.

- Place 2 tortillas on each piece of foil and top with steak, onions, and cilantro. Wrap each one up tightly and let rest 1 minute before serving.

Flank Steak or Flap Meat: Skirt steak is ideal for any carne asada preparation because it is flavorful, tender, and juicy. If skirt steak is not available, there are a other cuts of beef that give similar results. One of them is a popular cut of meat called flank steak. It is slightly thicker and chewier than skirt steak, but when cut into small pieces it is almost indiscernible. Another option is flap meat, which closely resembles skirt steak in texture but doesn't have quite as much flavor.

Keeping the Tacos Warm: To keep tacos warm for an extended period place them in a slow cooker set on low. Provide tongs to pull them out, as they may be hot. To keep the tacos warm 20 minutes or less, place the wrapped tacos in tortilla warmers until you are ready to serve them.

Preparing the Carne Asada

- Use a sharp knife to cut the steak; use a fork to hold the meat in place while you cut.

- Slice the meat into ½-inch thin strips with the grain of the meat.

- Then cut the strips crosswise, against the grain, into small bite-size pieces.

- The meat will cool quickly after being cut, so assemble the tacos immediately.

Wrapping the Tacos

- Let the tacos rest in the foil, because the hot meat helps steam the tortillas.

- Place 2 fresh corn tortillas in the center of the foil. Top them with the steak, onions, and cilantro.

- Quickly pull together 2 edges of the foil and wrap them around the taco.

- Tuck the remaining edges of foil around the taco and let it sit for 1 to 2 minutes before serving.

TACOS & TOSTADAS

FISH TACOS

These delicious tacos are stuffed with battered and fried chunks of flaky white fish

Tacos can be filled with a variety of ingredients and are a staple in a Mexican diet. Like Carne asado tacos, fish tacos are one of the most popular versions. They are a staple in Mexico's Baja region and San Diego.

Stuffed with battered and fried chunks of flaky white fish, fish tacos are a favorite for lunch and dinner meals, and for the many street vendors who sell them throughout the evening and early morning hours.

The golden fried fish combined with the corn tortilla makes for a delicious snack or full meal. Fish tacos are perfect with a drizzle of lime juice and garnished with a couple of lime wedges to enhance the flavor of the ingredients. *Yield: Serves 4*

Ingredients

2 large eggs

$1/2$ cup flour

3 tablespoons masa harina

$1/4$ teaspoon salt

$1/2$ cup Crema Agria

$1/4$ cup mayonnaise

$1/2$ cup heavy cream

2 teaspoons lemon juice

2 teaspoons hot chile sauce

2 pounds red snapper or other white flaky fish
cut into 2-inch pieces

1 cup cooking oil

12 corn tortillas

2 cups shredded green cabbage

1 cup fresh salsa

Lime wedges

Fish Tacos

- For the batter, whisk together eggs and then mix in the flour, masa harina, and salt.

- For the sause, whisk together the Crema Agria, mayonnaise, cream, lemon juice, and hot chile sauce.

- Heat oil to 375°F. Dip fish into batter and fry until golden; drain on paper towels.

- Place 3 pieces of fish on each tortilla; top with cabbage.

- Drizzle sauce on each taco; serve with salsa and lime wedges.

Grilled Fish Tacos: Squeeze fresh limes over 2 pounds red snapper fillets and sprinkle a pinch or two of salt over them. Heat a grill over medium heat and cook the fish until flaky and cooked through. Cut the grilled fish into 2-inch chunks and use in place of the battered fish.

Fish Choices: Red snapper is mild in flavor and has a firm yet flaky texture that is ideal for fish tacos. However, there are other fish that work well and can be used instead of red snapper. Any rockfish would make a good substitute, and tilapia is a nice choice with its mild flavor and somewhat flaky texture. Another choice is halibut, which has a very light and flaky texture and a mild flavor.

Mixing the Batter

- Beat the eggs until they are smooth and creamy. Room temperature eggs are easiest to work with.

- Combine the flour, masa, and salt before adding it to the eggs to ensure they are evenly distributed.

- Add the flour a little at a time, beating the mixture after each addition.

- Mix the batter until it is smooth. It should be slightly thinner than pancake batter.

Frying the Fish

- The oil is ready when you drop a bit of batter into it and it sizzles and rises to the top.

- Use a fork to pierce a piece of fish and dip it in the batter. Use another fork to push the fish into the oil.

- Fry the fish in batches, as overcrowding the pan can cause the fish pieces to stick together or the oil to drop in temperature.

- The fish is ready when it is golden brown and cooked through.

TACOS & TOSTADAS

CARNITAS TOSTADA

Caramelized onions and tender pork carnitas top a crispy flour shell

When the Spanish conquistadors introduced pork in the 1500s, the native Mexicans quickly incorporated it into their diet. Pork was easy and inexpensive to raise yet provided massive amounts of meat. People experimented with different ways to cook this new protein, but the method of slow cooking the pork until it fried in its own fat became a great way to turn a tough cut of meat into a tender and delicious meal.

Native Mexicans wasted nothing; even stale tortillas were not thrown away. They were toasted until crispy and then topped with a variety of native ingredients such as beans and vegetables. *Yield: Serves 4–6*

Ingredients

1 tablespoon cooking oil

3 medium white onions, thinly sliced

2 ounces piloncillo, roughly chopped

$1/2$ teaspoon cumin

$1/2$ teaspoon coriander

$1/2$ teaspoon salt

1 cup cooking oil

10 small flour tortillas

1 pound warm pork carnitas

1 cup Fresh Salsa Topping

$1/2$ cup cilantro leaves

$1/2$ cup crumbled Cotija

Carnitas Tostada

- Heat 1 tablespoon oil in a large saucepan over medium-low heat. Add the onions, piloncillo, cumin, coriander, and salt. Cook until onions begin to caramelize.

- Heat 1 cup oil over medium-high heat and fry each tortilla until it is crispy and golden. Drain on paper towels.

- Top each tortilla with the caramelized onions, carnitas, a spoonful of salsa, and a sprinkle of cilantro and Cotija.

Fresh Salsa Topping: Chop 2 plum tomatoes, discarding most of the liquid and seeds. Dice ¹/₂ small onion into ¹/₄-inch pieces, and peel and chop 1 garlic clove. Combine the tomatoes, onion, garlic, ¹/₄ cup chopped cilantro, 1 tablespoon hot chile sauce, 1 teaspoon vinegar, and a pinch salt and toss together. Cover and refrigerate a minimum of 30 minutes to allow the flavors to meld.

Cooking the Onions

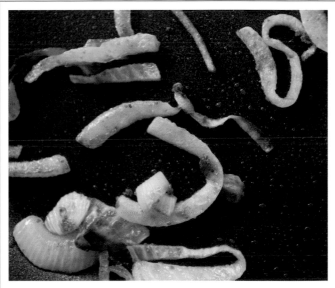

- The onions need to cook slowly in order for the sugars to caramelize and become golden.

- Keep the heat low and steady while you occasionally stir the onions.

- Make sure to flip the onions over to ensure even cooking.

- As they cook the onions will begin to wilt and become soft, and they will cook down to less than half their volume.

Frying the Tostada Shell

- Test the temperature of the pan by dropping a bit of tortilla in the oil. If it rises to the top, the pan is ready.

- One at a time carefully place a tortilla in the hot oil, cooking each side about 30 seconds.

- The tortilla will become golden and puff up when it is done. When you remove it from the heat, the puffiness will dissipate.

- Drain the tortillas between layers of paper towels. They will be fragile, so handle them carefully.

TACOS & TOSTADAS

SHREDDED BEEF TOSTADA

A crunchy corn tortilla is topped with succulent chunks of beef and sautéed vegetables

The Spaniards brought many New World foods back to Spain, but they also imported many Old World ingredients to Mexico, including beef, pork, citrus, dairy products, vinegar, and wine. The Mexicans incorporated these new ingredients into their traditional dishes and created techniques in order to utilize the new additions.

Topping a toasted tortilla with beans and other native ingredients was an everyday affair, and with the addition of hearty beef, each tostada became a rich and satisfying meal.

Shredded Beef Tostada includes tomatoes, onion, and smoky seasonings to create a flavorful fiesta. *Yield: Serves 6*

Ingredients

2 tablespoons cooking oil

1 red bell pepper, stems and seeds removed

1/2 small onion, chopped

1 plum tomato, chopped

3 tablespoons mild red chile sauce

1/2 teaspoon cumin

1 tablespoon ground chile powder

1/2 teaspoon salt

1 cup cooking oil

12 corn tortillas

1 cup prepared refried beans, heated

1 pound Easy Shredded Beef

1 cup shredded lettuce

1/2 cup salsa

1 cup crumbled queso fresco

Shredded Beef Tostada

- In a large saucepan heat 2 tablespoons oil over medium heat. Sauté the vegetables 5 minutes, until they begin to soften.

- Add the chile sauce and seasonings and cook 2 more minutes.

- In a medium saucepan heat 1 cup oil over medium high heat and fry each tortilla until crunchy. Drain on paper towels.

- Top each tortilla with a layer of refried beans, vegetable mixture, Easy Shredded Beef, lettuce, salsa, and cheese.

Easy Shredded Beef: In a large pot heat 1 tablespoon cooking oil over high heat and then add 1½ pounds beef chuck roast. Sear the outside of the roast on all sides just until it begins to brown and crisp up. Add enough water to cover the roast, as well as 1 4-ounce can chipotle chiles in adobo sauce and 2 garlic cloves. Cover and simmer 6 to 7 hours, until the meat is fork-tender. Drain the liquid and pull the beef into chunks, discarding any fat or gristle.

Cooking the Vegetables

- Make sure the pan is hot before adding the vegetables so they don't absorb too much oil.

- Add the vegetables slowly and carefully so the moisture in them doesn't cause hot oil to splatter.

- Stir and flip the vegetables often to be sure they cook evenly.

- You want the vegetables to be slightly soft but not mushy.

Assembling the Tostadas

- To ensure each tostada gets an equal amount of ingredients, lay the tortillas on platters or baking sheets and top them one layer at a time.

- Prepare the tostadas immediately after the toppings are ready so they don't get cold.

- You can also serve them buffet style and provide the toppings in separate bowls so that everyone can customize his or her own tostada.

TACOS & TOSTADAS

VEGETARIAN TOSTADA

This tostada is very satisfying, with beans, tomatoes, and shredded cheese

Native Mexicans subsisted on a mainly vegetarian diet of beans, squash, corn, tomatoes, and chiles. Many traditional Mexican dishes are vegetarian, such as the stuffed chile dish called chiles rellenos. Beef and pork were introduced in the 1500s, but the native Mexican diet was already rooted in a vegetarian cuisine.

You don't have to be a vegetarian to enjoy the flavors of this delicious tostada topped with earthy black beans and juicy tomatoes seasoned with smoky cumin and grassy oregano. The softness of the beans and tomatoes is a nice contrast to the crunchy corn tortilla and rich, melted cheese. Enjoy this tostada for lunch or dinner or as a snack. *Yield: Serves 6*

Ingredients

1 tablespoon cooking oil

1 onion, chopped

3 garlic cloves, crushed

2 cups black beans, cooked and drained

3 tomatoes, seeded and diced

$^{1}/_{2}$ cup chile sauce

$^{1}/_{2}$ teaspoon cumin

1 teaspoon oregano

$^{1}/_{4}$ teaspoon salt

1 cup oil

12 corn tortillas

1 cup shredded queso Manchego

$^{3}/_{4}$ cup fresh salsa

$^{3}/_{4}$ cup sour cream

Vegetarian Tostada

- In a large saucepan heat 1 tablespoon oil over medium heat; sauté the onion and garlic 2 minutes. Add the beans and begin to mash them as they cook.

- Add the tomatoes, chile sauce, and seasonings and cook another 5 minutes, until the mixture is heated and thickened.

- In a large saucepan heat 1 cup oil over medium high heat; fry each tortilla until crunchy. Drain on paper towels.

- Top each tortilla with beans, cheese, salsa, and sour cream.

Pinto Bean and Green Chile Tostadas: Switch out the black beans for the pinto beans for a mild and delicious earthy flavor. Replace the tomatoes with three roasted Anaheim chiles chopped into $1/2$-inch pieces. Use $1/2$ cup salsa verde in place of the chile sauce.

If you don't have fresh tomatoes, use a 14-ounce can of canned tomatoes. Make sure they are not already seasoned with basil or oregano. And if you do not have cooked black beans, a 15-ounce can will do. Rinse and drain the beans before using them.

Frying the Tortillas

Assembling the Tostada

- Make sure the oil is sufficiently heated before frying the tortillas. You can test this by pinching off a small piece of tortilla and dropping it into the oil. If it sizzles and rises to the top, the oil is ready.

- The tortillas should be crispy and golden. If you overcook them, they will become hard.

- Drain the tortillas on paper towels in a single layer, then add another paper towel and another layer of tortillas. Repeat with the remaining tortillas.

- Use a light hand when spreading the beans onto the tostada shell so that you don't crack it.

- The beans need to be thick enough so that the next layer sticks to them.

- Assemble the ingredients onto the tostadas as soon as the tortillas are ready.

- You can serve the tostadas already assembled, or provide the ingredients and let diners assemble their own.

TACOS & TOSTADAS

HUEVOS RANCHEROS

Sunny-side up eggs on a corn tortilla topped with ranchero sauce makes a hearty breakfast

Born from the need to have a hearty breakfast without sacrificing flavor, these ranch-style eggs are a delicious and hearty breakfast of fried eggs served on top of a crisp corn tortilla and smothered with a zesty ranchero sauce. Refried beans, avocados, and chiles are often served along side the egg dish.

There are as many recipes for huevos rancheros as there are chefs. The traditional versions all begin with eggs served on tortillas with a tomato-based sauce. Some people like to add cheese or additional hot chile sauce. *Yield: Serves 2*

Ingredients

¼ cup cooking oil

4 corn tortillas

4 extra-large eggs

1 cup prepared refried beans (homemade or canned)

Salt to taste

Ranchero Sauce

Huevos Rancheros

- In a small frying pan heat the oil over medium-high heat and cook each tortilla 1 minute on each side, until crispy and golden. Drain on paper towels.

- Drain most of the oil from the pan and return pan to medium-low heat. Slowly cook each egg on one side

- until whites are firm but yolks are runny.

- Spread the refried beans over each tortilla and place one egg on top of each. Add salt to taste.

- Smother with hot Ranchero Sauce and let sit 10 seconds before serving.

Ranchero Sauce: Heat 2 tablespoons oil and sauté 2 garlic cloves, 1 seeded and diced serrano or jalpeño chile, and ¼ cup onion 3 minutes. Reduce heat and add 3 cups diced plum tomatoes. Cook about 5 or 6 minutes, until tomatoes become wilted, slightly mashing the ingredients together as they cook. Add 1 tablespoon oregano, ½ teaspoon ground chile, and salt to taste; simmer about 5 minutes more.

Cooking the Eggs and Ingredients

- Make sure the pan is not too hot when you add the eggs. Remove it from the heat if necessary. Cook the eggs over low heat so the whites have time to cook without being flipped.

- Place a lid over the eggs so steam can help cook the whites, but watch carefully so it doesn't cook the yolks too.

- Use a spatula to slide under the yolk portion so that you don't break them while moving them to the plate.

- In the meantime, simmer the tomatoes to soften and start the sauce.

Preparing the Sauce

- After the ingredients for the sauce have begun to cook through and soften, use the back of a spoon to mash them together.

- The sauce should have some texture, but it should not be overly chunky.

- For a smooth sauce use a handheld stick blender until the desired consistency is reached.

- The sauce should be wet but not watery. If there is too much liquid, turn up the heat until the liquid cooks off.

BREAKFAST DISHES

CHILAQUILES

This quick and easy recipe is made with stale corn tortillas cooked in a green chile sauce

This dish is a traditional Mexican meal and is a great way to use up stale tortillas or tortilla chips. The tortillas are fried until crispy and then cooked in a green chile sauce.

Regional variations are common, including using a red chile sauce instead of green. They are usually eaten for breakfast or lunch and are quick and easy to make.

Chilaquiles can easily be elevated to a more substantial meal with the addition of some sort of protein such as chicken or eggs. Even though it is thought of as a breakfast dish, you can serve it up anytime. *Yield: Serves 4*

Ingredients

10 stale tortillas

¼ cup oil

¼ teaspoon salt

2 cups green chile sauce

1 cup shredded Queso Quesadilla

½ cup sour cream

½ cup chopped onion

½ cup chopped cilantro

Lime wedges for garnish

Chilaquiles

- Cut tortillas in half and then into 1-inch strips. Separate so they are not stuck together.

- In a large pan, heat the oil over medium-high heat and fry the tortilla strips. Sprinkle salt over the top.

- Reduce heat to low and carefully pour in the chile sauce. Simmer the strips in the sauce until they are softened.

- Turn the heat off, sprinkle the cheese on top, and allow it to melt. Serve with sour cream, onion, cilantro, and lime wedges.

Stale Tortilla Chips: Chilaquiles are an excellent way to use up stale tortillas and you can also use stale tortilla chips with excellent results. Just use them in place of the stale tortillas but do not add any additional salt. Keep in mind that you will need to use actual tortilla chips, not corn chips which are an entirely different thing.

Chicken Chilaquiles: Chilaquiles are not only a great way to use up stale tortillas, they are also a great way to use up leftover chicken. Shred leftover chicken or cut it into bite-size pieces. Cook the tortillas first, just until they begin to get crispy, then add the chicken to warm it up while the tortillas continue to crisp.

Cooking the Strips in the Sauce

- As soon as the sauce is heated through, begin checking the strips for doneness. You want the tortilla strips tender, not soggy.

- If they are not soft enough keep the sauce at a slow simmer, stirring occasionally.

- When the strips are nearly ready, remove the pan from heat and top with the cheese. The dish will continue to cook in the hot pan for a minute or two even without the heat.

Preparing the Cheese

- Queso Quesadilla has a soft, creamy texture and is considered a melting cheese.

- Because it is so soft, be careful not to press it too hard when shredding it or it may clog the shredder blade.

- Keep the grated cheese in a cool, dry area until ready to use.

- To speed up the melting process, you can cover the pan for a minute after you add the Queso Quesadilla.

BREAKFAST DISHES

HUEVOS CON MACHACA

Light and fluffy scrambled eggs with chunks of flavorful beef and juicy tomatoes

Chicken eggs are not a native Mexican ingredient. Turkey and quail ran free, but their eggs were hard to come by. So eggs were not really used in the native Mexican diet. The Spaniards, who introduced many new and exciting ingredients to Mexico, introduced chickens. Along with chickens came chicken eggs, which have become a staple ingredient.

Machaca is an ingredient common in the arid northern regions of Mexico, where ranchers came up with a way to dry marinated meat similar to beef jerky. But machaca has a shredded texture and stronger flavor than standard jerky. This dried meat could sustain them on the ranch, where food was scarce. *Yield: Serves 4*

Ingredients

2 tablespoons lard

$^1/_2$ small onion, coarsely chopped

$^1/_2$ serrano chile, finely chopped

1 cup Machaca

1 plum tomato, seeded and diced

Pinch cumin

Pinch salt

8 eggs, beaten

Huevos con Machaca

- Melt the lard in a large skillet. Sauté the onion and chile about 1 minute.

- Add the machaca, tomato, and seasonings. Cook another 5 minutes; remove and set aside.

- In the same pan, cook the eggs, constantly stirring and scraping with a wooden spoon or spatula to scramble them.

- When the eggs are almost done, remove from heat and fold in tomato and machaca mixture. Let eggs sit in the hot pan an additional minute to finish cooking.

ZOOM

Machaca can also be a shredded beef dish, which is more moist than dried meat. Dried machaca can be found in most Mexican markets or you can make your own machaca and adjust the cooking times for a drier or more moist result.

• • • • • **RECIPE VARIATION** • • • •

Green Chile Huevos con Machaca: For a delicious and tangy flavor, use chiles in place of the tomato. Choose 1 or 2 chiles, such as poblano or hatch. Char them until the skins bubble and turn black. Place them in an airtight container 2 minutes. Peel off the charred skin, remove the stem, and scrape out the seeds. Chop the chiles and use them in place of the tomato.

Cooking the Eggs

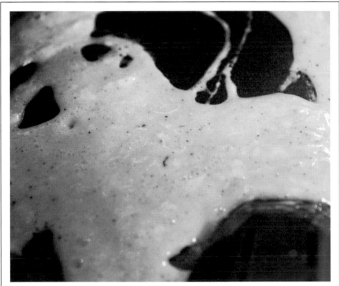

- The pan must be hot enough before you pour in the eggs or they will not become fluffy.

- Continuously scrape the sides and bottom of the pan to incorporate the cooked and raw areas.

- Some browned bits leftover from cooking the other ingredients may end up in the eggs. The bits add flavor to the eggs.

- You can also cook the eggs in a separate pan if you prefer.

Finishing the Eggs

- Let the eggs cook about 75 percent before adding the other ingredients. The eggs should be firming up yet still quite moist on the outside.

- If you add the other ingredients too soon, the eggs will just coat the ingredients and become mushy.

- After you add the ingredients, carefully fold them into the eggs. You don't want to stir it or have too firm a hand or you will break the eggs up.

BREAKFAST DISHES

HUEVOS CON CHORIZO

Hot and spicy chorizo cooked with eggs and topped with sour cream is an eye-opener

Eggs are popular in Mexico, with the average person consuming 300 eggs per year. It's no wonder there are plenty of egg recipes to liven up your morning meal. Scrambled eggs are a quick and easy way to prepare eggs, and the chorizo adds a delicious spicy flavor to the dish. Green chiles naturally go well with chorizo, and they bring in a tangy flavor to contrast the heavier sausage. Because of the high amounts of protein between the sausage and eggs, this is a meal that will keep you satisfied all morning long. *Yield: Serves 2–3*

Ingredients

¹/₂ pound Mexican chorizo

1 4-ounce can diced green chiles

1 teaspoon cooking oil

6 eggs, beaten

1 teaspoon cilantro leaves, finely chopped

1 green onion, sliced

¹/₂ cup crumbled cotija

¹/₂ avocado, cut into 8 slices

¹/₄ cup sour cream

Huevos con Chorizo

- In a medium pan begin to brown the chorizo. Add the green chiles and cook until chorizo is cooked through and crumbled.

- Pour cooking oil into a large pan. Pour eggs into pan, constantly stirring to scramble.

- When eggs are almost done, fold in the cooked chorizo and chiles, cilantro, and onion. Remove from heat.

- Sprinkle cheese over the top. Let it sit in the warm pan 2 minutes to melt. Garnish with avocado slices and sour cream.

• • • • RECIPE VARIATIONS • • • •

Spanish Chorizo: Mexican chorizo is a raw sausage made with heavily seasoned ground pork. Spanish chorizo is a cured sausage that is seasoned with paprika, which gives it a bright red hue. While it is a totally different type of sausage, you can use it in place of Mexican chorizo to add flavor and color to Huevos con Chorizo. Cut the Spanish chorizo into ¼-inch pieces and cook them just long enough to heat through; prepare the recipe as directed.

Precook the Chorizo: To cut down on cooking time in the morning, cook the chorizo the night before. Brown the sausage until it is crumbly and cooked through. Drain it on paper towels and let cool completely. Store it in the refrigerator in a covered container until ready for use. Reheat the sausage in a pan over medium heat until warmed through.

Cooking the Chorizo

- Remove the chorizo from any casings it may come in.

- Use the back of the cooking utensil to mash the chorizo into the pan and cook until it is crumbly.

- The sausage is cooked when it is thoroughly browned and no pink remains.

- Drain the chorizo on paper towels to remove excess fat.

Adding the Chorizo

- The eggs are nearly done when they are firm yet still have a slightly moist coating on them.

- Fold in the chorizo and green chiles, cilantro, and onion.

- Avoid using a stirring motion or the eggs will break apart and overmix with the chorizo mixture.

- Serve immediately, as the eggs do not reheat well.

MOLLETES
Beans and cheese top toasted slices of crusty Mexican bread

These little pieces of crisp, toasted bread smothered with beans and cheese and baked until bubbling make a nearly perfect breakfast or snack. They are a great way to use up leftover beans from dinner the night before, as well as a great use of any bread you need to use up.

Bolillos are delicious Mexican rolls that are crunchy and golden brown on the outside and soft and chewy on the inside. They toast well while maintaining their chewy texture.

The term molletes is often misinterpreted to mean "muffins" or sometimes "cookies." But real molletes fresh out of the oven are much better for you and make a more filling breakfast than a muffin or cookie would. *Yield: Serves 4–6*

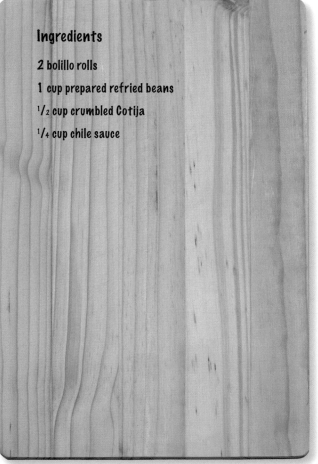

Ingredients

2 bolillo rolls

1 cup prepared refried beans

$^1/_2$ cup crumbled Cotija

$^1/_4$ cup chile sauce

Molletes

- Preheat oven to 400°F.

- Cut each bolillo into 5 or 6 slices. Place on a baking sheet and toast in the oven 3 minutes.

- Spread each slice with refried beans and a sprinkle of Cotija. Return to the oven and bake 3 minutes, until the edges are golden brown and beans are heated through.

- Top with a drizzle of chile sauce; serve immediately.

Molletes Dulce: Although molletes are traditionally a savory dish, a sweet version can also be made. Toast the bollillos as directed and top with butter, a drizzle of honey, and a light sprinkle of Cotija. Bake until cheese is golden and melted. Another sweet option is to smear the toasted bolillos with a lightly sweet fruit jam and bake until the jam is warmed and bubbly.

French Bread: Bolillos are very similar to French bread, with its golden brown, crusty exterior and moist, chewy interior. So if bolillos are not available, substitute French bread. Cut it into slices and then cut the slices in half.

Baking the Bolillo

Topping the Molletes

- Place the bread slices in a single layer on an ungreased baking sheet.

- The slices should have at least ½ inch space between them to ensure even cooking.

- Toast the bread until it becomes golden. You want it to be toasted on the outside but still soft in the middle. If you overcook the pieces they will be too crunchy, almost like a crouton.

- Spread a thin layer of beans, about ¼-inch thick, over each slice with a spatula.

- Sprinkle the Cotija over the layer of beans. If the beans are stiff, pat the cheese gently into it so it sticks.

- The Cotija will melt and become golden, but it will hold its shape.

- The Molletes are ready when the beans and cheese begin to bubble.

BREAKFAST DISHES

BREAKFAST BURRITO

Stuff a soft flour tortilla with sizzling chorizo, fluffy eggs, and zesty salsa

Breakfast burritos are an easy and convenient way to enjoy a breakfast on the go. They are usually filled with a combination of breakfast items, with the most popular being eggs, sausage, and salsa.

The burrito, which is popular in the far northern regions of Mexico, is not widely known outside the cities near the U.S. border. But the residents of those northern cities known for their burritos enjoy them anytime of day. This breakfast version includes the flavors of a hearty morning meal within a portable, edible package. *Yield: Serves 4*

Ingredients

1 pound Mexican Chorizo

8 eggs, beaten

Salt to taste

4 large flour tortillas, warmed

1 cup shredded queso quesadilla

$1/2$ cup salsa

$1/2$ cup Crema Agria

Breakfast Burritos

- Preheat oven to 400°F.

- In a small pan, cook the chorizo over medium heat until cooked through. Drain excess fat. Remove chorizo from pan; set aside.

- Return pan to medium heat. Pour eggs into pan and cook, constantly stir-ring to scramble. Add salt to taste.

- Place chorizo and eggs down the center of each tortilla and top with shredded cheese, salsa, and Crema Agria. Fold the burrito and let sit about 1 minute to let the cheese melt.

Steak and Eggs: Use leftover carne asada instead of the sausage. Cut the carne asada into bite-size pieces and heat over medium heat until warmed through. Add it to the eggs as directed.

Cheese Substitutions: If you don't have any Queso Quesadilla, use Monterey Jack instead. Monterey Jack has a tangier flavor, but overall it is a fine substitute and will make a delicious burrito.

Heating the Tortillas

- A soft, warm tortilla is much easier to fold than a cold, stiff one.

- Heat each tortilla briefly on a comal to soften it and give it a fresh cooked flavor.

- Make the burrito immediately after the tortilla comes off the comal so the tortilla is still warm and pliable.

- If you need to, you can keep the warm tortillas on a plate under a towel to keep them warm.

Assembling the Burritos

- Place the ingredients in a line down the middle of the tortilla, leaving 2 inches of space at either end.

- Layer the ingredients neatly so you get a little of each in each bite.

- Fold one edge over the filling and then fold the bottom and top over. Fold the final edge over and let the burrito rest on the seam.

- Let the burrito rest a minute to allow it to mold to the fillings; this will help it stay closed.

BREAKFAST DISHES

PINTO BEANS

These traditional beans have a subtle earthy flavor and make an excellent side dish

Beans are native to Mexico and have been a staple in the Mexican diet for thousands of years. They provide protein and fiber, which are integral parts of a healthy diet. They also contain valuable nutrients, vitamins, and complex carbohydrates.

Because they are naturally inexpensive, beans have gotten a bad reputation as being food for the poor, but more recently they are being praised for their nutritional content and ease of preparation.

Pinto beans are the main ingredient for refried beans, but they are also delicious when served as whole beans. *Yield: Serves 8–10*

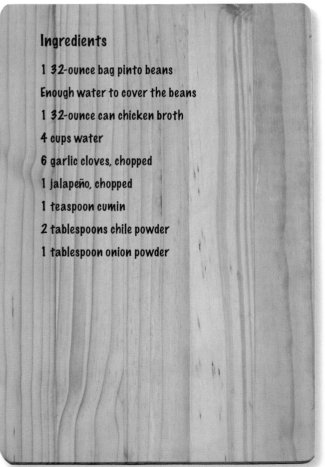

Ingredients

1 32-ounce bag pinto beans

Enough water to cover the beans

1 32-ounce can chicken broth

4 cups water

6 garlic cloves, chopped

1 jalapeño, chopped

1 teaspoon cumin

2 tablespoons chile powder

1 tablespoon onion powder

Pinto Beans

- Rinse the beans and pick out any debris. Put the beans in a large pot or bowl, cover with water, and let soak overnight.

- Drain the liquid and discard. Rinse the beans and place into a large pot.

- Add the chicken broth, water, garlic, jalapeño, and seasonings to the beans and bring to a simmer.

- Cover the beans and simmer 6 hours. Uncover and let simmer until liquid reduces to a slightly thickened broth.

• • • • RECIPE VARIATIONS • • • •

Using Canned Beans: Homemade pinto beans have a firm texture and a hearty flavor that is easily distinguishable from the canned variety. However, if you are going to use canned beans, you can spice them up to add some flavor. Bring the beans to a simmer with the chopped garlic, jalapeño, and seasonings called for in the recipe. Simmer 15 minutes and serve.

Spicy Pinto Beans: Instead of the jalapeño, use 2 chopped serrano chiles to take the heat from mild to medium. Add up to 1 tablespoon of your favorite hot chile sauce to add even more flavor and kick up the heat a notch.

Soaking the Beans

- Make sure you cover the beans with adequate water, as they will swell while soaking.

- The beans can be left at room temperature overnight to allow them to soften.

- Do not leave them out longer than overnight or they may begin to go bad.

- It is normal for the water to have small bubbles around the edges after soaking.

Simmering the Beans

- As the beans simmer, the liquid should cook down to form a thick broth.

- Turn the heat up if the liquid is still too thin when the beans are nearly done.

- If the heat is too high, the liquid may cook off before the beans are ready. If that happens, add 1 or 2 cups boiling water. Do not add cool water, as it will slow the cooking process.

REFRIED BEANS

These tasty beans are mashed and fried, which gives them their signature texture and flavor

Refried beans are often served as a side dish topped with a sprinkle of Cotija cheese, but they can also be used as a filling for burritos or a topping for tostadas.

The word refried would suggest that somehow the beans are fried once and then a second time, but that is not the case. The Mexican term for refried beans is actually *frijoles refritos*, which translates into "well-fried beans." The term refritos was mistranslated into refried and the term stuck.

Refried beans are typically made with pinto beans, but just about any bean can be used, including black, pink, or red beans. The cooked beans are mashed and fried until they have a slightly creamy texture and loads of flavor. *Yield: Serves 8–10*

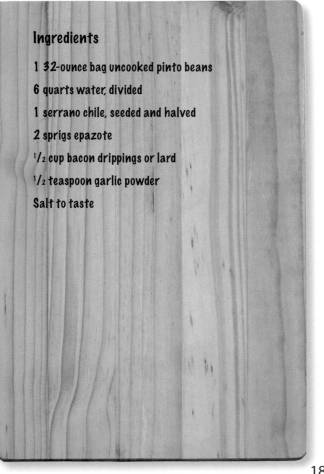

Ingredients

1 32-ounce bag uncooked pinto beans

6 quarts water, divided

1 serrano chile, seeded and halved

2 sprigs epazote

1/2 cup bacon drippings or lard

1/2 teaspoon garlic powder

Salt to taste

Refried Beans

- Rinse beans and check for debris. Soak overnight in 2 quarts water.

- After soaking, place the beans in a large pot with 4 quarts water, the serrano, and the epazote. Simmer 8 hours, until extremely soft.

- Melt the lard on a large comal over medium-high heat. In batches, fry the beans and mash them onto the pan. Remove from pan and repeat with another batch. Add garlic powder and salt.

• • • • RECIPE VARIATION • • • •

Refried Black Beans: While pinto beans are the traditional bean for refried beans, use the technique in the recipe to fry other bean varieties as well. Black beans are usually served in their whole form, but their strong earthy flavor lends itself to the rich texture brought out by frying them.

ZOOM

Canned refried beans are often thick, paste-like substances that have very little flavor. If your only option is canned refried beans, fix them up. First add water $1/4$ cup at a time to thin the beans out so they are not so stiff. Then simmer them with some chopped onion, garlic, and jalapeño to add some flavor.

Frying the Beans

- Heat the lard over medium heat 1 to 2 minutes, until it has melted.

- Place a spoonful of beans onto the hot comal and mash them into the hot lard as they fry. When the beans have reached the desired texture, remove them to a bowl; set aside.

- Place another spoonful of beans on the comal and repeat the process until all the beans have been mashed and fried.

Seasoning the Beans

- Transfer the beans to a mixing bowl when they are done frying.

- Sprinkle the garlic powder and salt over the top of the freshly fried beans.

- Fold the garlic and salt into the bean mixture, being careful not to mash the beans too much more.

- Enjoy the beans immediately, or let them cool and store them in the refrigerator in a covered container up to 3 days.

BLACK BEANS

Black beans are a delicious side dish and make a great filling for burritos

The black bean is another popular bean enjoyed in the Mexican diet. It originated over 7,000 years ago in the southern region of Mexico and was eaten by the native Mexicans as an excellent source of protein and nutrients.

Black beans can be used to make delicious soups and sauces and they are often served as a side dish in their inky broth. Black beans are most popular in Southern Mexico, and they have spread in popularity and are now consumed throughout the Carribean and United States in many dishes.

Black beans are well suited to many preparations but they are most delicious when enjoyed simply as dish of slow-cooked beans. *Yield: Serves 8–10*

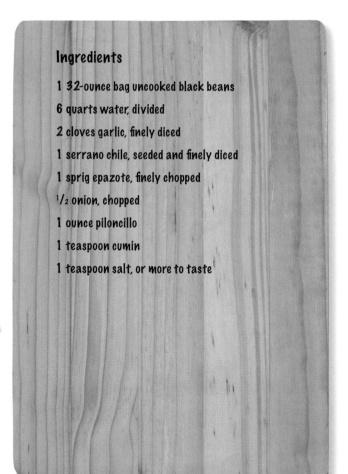

Ingredients

1 32-ounce bag uncooked black beans

6 quarts water, divided

2 cloves garlic, finely diced

1 serrano chile, seeded and finely diced

1 sprig epazote, finely chopped

1/2 onion, chopped

1 ounce piloncillo

1 teaspoon cumin

1 teaspoon salt, or more to taste

Black Beans

- Sort through the beans to check for any debris. Rinse and soak them overnight in 2 quarts water.

- After soaking, place beans in a large pot and cover with 4 quarts water. Bring beans to a boil, reduce to a simmer, and cook 4 hours.

- Add remaining ingredients and simmer another 2 hours, until beans are soft and a broth has formed.

• • • • RECIPE VARIATIONS • • • •

Sweet Black Beans: Instead of just 1 ounce piloncillo, use 16 ounces. Chop the piloncillo with a serrated knife before adding it. You can serve Sweet Black Beans anywhere you'd serve a side dish of beans.

Smoky and Zesty Black Beans: Add 2 teaspoons ground cumin to create a powerful smoky flavor. Add an additional serrano chile to kick up the heat. For a tangy flavor, include a roasted green chile chopped into bite-size pieces.

Preparing Beans for Cooking

- After the beans are done soaking, you can rinse them to remove any additional starches.

- Rinse them with cool water at least 1 minute, using your fingers to move them around to ensure they are evenly rinsed.

- Keep an eye out for any remaining debris and remove it.

- It is okay if some of the skin comes off some of the beans. Just leave them and continue with the recipe.

Simmering the Beans

- If the liquid cooks off too fast, add additional boiling water about 1 cup at a time and reduce the heat.

- If the beans are done but the broth isn't thick enough, there may be too much liquid. Just turn the heat up so the liquid cooks off quickly.

- The finished beans should have a slightly thickened broth that sticks to the beans if you use a slotted spoon.

MEXICAN RICE

This dish gets its flavor from chicken broth, tomato sauce, and garlic and onions

Mexican rice is a popular dish in central and northern Mexico, where the dried grains of rice are toasted with garlic and onions and then cooked in a mixture of chicken stock, tomatoes, and sometimes chiles. This method gives the rice its delicious flavor and unique texture. The addition of tomatoes or red chiles provides the signature reddish brown color.

Mexican rice makes a great side dish and is sometimes used as a filling for burritos. In Mexico it is simply known as *arroz,* which means "rice," and in the United States it is commonly known as Spanish rice. *Yield: Serves 4–6*

Ingredients

3 garlic cloves, finely chopped

¼ medium onion

2 tablespoons cooking oil

1½ cups rice

2½ cups chicken broth

1 cup tomato sauce

4 heaping tablespoons finely chopped parsley (optional)

Mexican Rice

- Sauté the garlic and onion in the oil over medium heat 2 to 3 minutes, until onions are softened.

- Add rice and stir about 5 minutes, until rice becomes a golden brown color.

- Carefully add broth and tomato sauce; stir and bring to a boil. Once mixture starts to boil, turn heat to low and cover; simmer 20 minutes.

- Fluff the rice with a fork and fold in the parsley. Serve immediately.

• • • • RECIPE VARIATIONS • • • •

Substitutions: If you don't have fresh garlic or onions, use the equivalent in powder form. Do not sauté the powder, just add it when you add the liquids. If you don't have tomato sauce, use unseasoned stewed tomatoes or canned diced tomatoes with the liquid.

Spicy Mexican Rice with Chile: To add an extra layer of smoky flavor, add a tablespoon of finely chopped chipotle chile with the tomato sauce. Or fold in a tablespoon of your favorite hot chile sauce after the rice has cooked.

Sautéing the Rice

- Heat the oil before adding the onion to the pan.

- Let the onion cook 1 minute before adding the garlic, as the garlic has a tendency to burn quickly.

- When the onion is softened and the garlic becomes golden, add the rice.

- The rice will become opaque and begin to turn golden when it is ready for the addition of the liquid.

Cooking the Rice

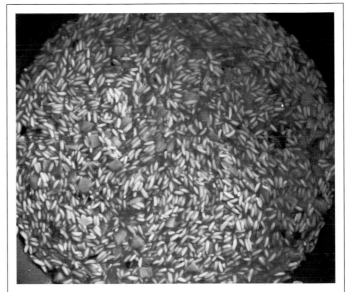

- Be careful when you add the broth to the rice. Pour it in very slowly at first to avoid splattering hot oil.

- Once the liquid is in, keep the heat at medium, wait for it to come to a simmer, and then reduce the heat to maintain the simmer.

- Keep the rice covered while it cooks. Do not open the lid or the steam will be released. Check the rice at 20 minutes. It should be soft but easily fluffed with a fork.

MEXICAN WHITE RICE

Fluffy white rice with peas, carrots, and green chiles makes a flavorful side dish

White rice is popular all over Mexico but more so in the southern regions. It is prepared simply by toasting it with onions and garlic and simmering it in water or chicken broth. The resulting rice is fluffy and flavorful.

It is common to add vegetables to the rice, which add additional flavor and color. They can be selected for the dish itself,

but more often whatever vegetables are on hand are added to the rice.

You can serve Mexican White Rice as a side dish or use it in soups, stews, and other preparations. *Yield: Serves 6*

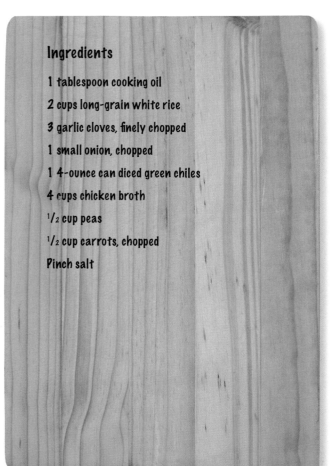

Ingredients

1 tablespoon cooking oil

2 cups long-grain white rice

3 garlic cloves, finely chopped

1 small onion, chopped

1 4-ounce can diced green chiles

4 cups chicken broth

1/2 cup peas

1/2 cup carrots, chopped

Pinch salt

Mexican White Rice

- In a large saucepan heat the oil over medium-high heat and add the rice, garlic, onion, and chiles.

- Sauté over medium heat until the rice starts to brown slightly, about 5 minutes. Add the broth,

- vegetables, and salt; bring to a boil.

- Cover and reduce heat to low; simmer 20 minutes.

- Remove rice from heat and fluff with a fork. Serve immediately.

• • • • RECIPE VARIATIONS • • • •

Mexican White Rice with Corn: For even more color and flavor you can add ¹/₂ cup corn when you add the other vegetables.

Medium-Grain Rice: This dish is also delicious with medium-grain rice, which is a stickier variety when cooked, but adds flavor and a unique texture to the finished dish. If you use medium-grain rice, soak it overnight and thoroughly rinse it before cooking.

Cooking the Rice

- The rice cooks at first in the simmering water and then finishes in the pressurized steam that develops as the water simmers.

- It is important to keep the rice covered while it cooks

  to keep the steam and pressure inside the pot.

- If you need to take the lid off for any reason, add 1 tablespoon hot water to the pot to replace the lost moisture.

Fluffing the Rice

- Use a fork in a scraping motion across the top of the rice. It should begin to separate and fluff up.

- The grains of rice should be light and easy to move around; they should not be sticky or mushy.

- If the rice is still dry or crunchy, add 2 tablespoons of hot water, cover, and return to low heat 5 minutes, until the rice is cooked through.

ESQUITES

A popular street snack in Mexico, these grilled corn kernels are simple yet addictive

Esquites are simply kernels of corn cooked in lard or butter, but it's the method by which they are cooked that creates their signature roasted flavor. Sometimes sausage, onions, lime juice, or other flavorings are added to the corn snack to add taste and texture. But most often people enjoy just the corn itself.

Street vendors sell esquites, serving them up in convenient cups to be eaten as a snack while you carry on with your day. Toppings such as chile powder, salt, and pepper are provided to customize the esquites to your own taste. *Yield: Serves 4*

Ingredients

4 ears fresh corn

¹/₂ cup water

¹/₄ cup fresh butter

¹/₄ teaspoon salt

Esquites

- Remove husks and excess strings from the corn. Cut the corn kernels off the cob.

- In a large saucepan, heat the water over medium-high heat. Add the corn and cook until the water evaporates and the corn has softened.

- Add the butter and salt and fry the corn over high heat 3 to 4 minutes, until it begins to brown. Serve immediately.

190

ZOOM

While juicy corn kernels topped with melted butter are hard to improve upon, there is another street food also made with corn. It is called elote, which is roasted corn on the cob served on a stick. It is eaten almost like a Popsicle. To make your own elote, sprinkle salt over fresh ears of corn and grill until they become soft and golden brown.

Toppings for Esquites: There are a variety of toppings to personalize Esquites to your own taste. Try squeezing on lemon juice or adding a dollop of Crema Agria. A sprinkle of cheese adds flavor and texture as does a sprinkle of chile powder.

Removing the Corn

- Use a sharp knife to cut a small portion off the widest end of the cob. This will allow the cob to stand on end without slipping.

- Slide your knife down the cob between the kernels and the hard center. Repeat on each side until all the kernels have been removed.

- Do not use a serrated knife or a sawing motion, as it may tear the kernels apart.

Cooking Esquites

- After adding the water to the pan, keep the temperature at a point where the kernels have 2 to 3 minutes to cook before the water cooks off.

- Use the freshest butter possible for the best-tasting results.

- The corn is done when it begins to brown slightly around the edges, yet the kernels are still full and robust.

- If you overcook the corn, the kernels will begin to wilt and become wrinkly.

191

POTATO & CHEESE QUESADILLA

These golden brown pockets of melted cheese and roasted potatoes are just about the perfect snack

Masa, which is ground corn that has been treated to remove its hulls, is most often used to create little flat disks cooked to create a tortilla. Before you cook the tortilla, you can add a few fillings, fold the tortilla in half, and then cook it to create a traditional quesadilla.

The most flavorful cooking method is to fry the quesadillas until they are crispy and golden brown, but they can also be toasted on a hot comal.

Potatoes and cheese create a common filling, as do combinations of cheese, chiles, and chorizo. Exotic ingredients such as squash blossoms or huitlacoche can also be used to stuff quesadillas. *Yield: Serves 4–6*

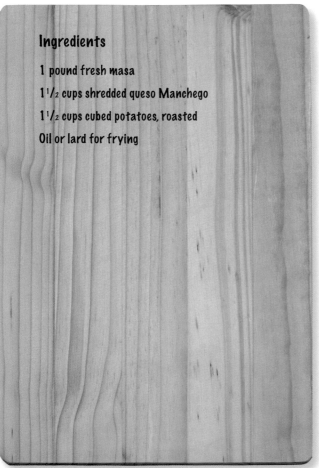

Ingredients

1 pound fresh masa

1 1/2 cups shredded queso Manchego

1 1/2 cups cubed potatoes, roasted

Oil or lard for frying

Potato and Cheese Quesadilla

- Divide the masa into 10 balls. Roll each ball between two pieces of cellophane or on a floured surface to about 4 inches across.

- Place equal amounts of cheese and roasted potatoes onto each piece of masa.

- Fold tortilla in half and press edges with a fork to seal.

- Fry in hot oil until golden brown and crispy. Drain the finished tortillas on paper towels. Serve immediately.

Chicken and Green Chile: Chicken and green chiles make an excellent combination for traditional fried quesadillas. Use freshly cooked chicken or leftovers. Toss 1 cup cooked chicken, 1 cup shredded queso Manchego, $1/2$ cup green chile sauce, and $1/4$ cup roasted green chile cut into small pieces. Use the filling in place of the potatoes and cheese.

Masa Harina: If you don't have fresh masa, use masa harina. Add 1 cup warm water to a scant 2 cups masa harina and mix them together until a dough forms. Knead the dough 2 minutes and use as directed.

Roasting the Potatoes

- Place the potatoes on a lightly greased baking sheet.

- Spread them out in a single layer; be sure they are touching as little as possible.

- Place in a 350°F oven about 30 minutes, occasionally tossing the potatoes.

- When they are done cooking, the potatoes should be golden brown on the outside and soft on the inside.

Frying the Quesadillas

- After filling the quesadillas, heat the oil over medium heat. Drop a pinch of the masa into the oil. If it sizzles and rises to the top, the oil is ready.

- Using a spoon, carefully slide the quesadillas into the oil. Do not drop them

in, as the oil will splatter.

- Fry in batches of 2 or 3 quesadillas at a time.

- Drain the fried quesadillas on paper towels to absorb excess oil. Serve immediately.

BEAN & CHEESE BURRITO

This classic burrito is stuffed with smooth refried beans and gooey melted cheese

The burrito, which was made popular in the border city of Juarez, Mexico, has evolved to include a multitude of fillings. Authentic burritos found in Juarez are small and thin and filled with meat and cheese and sometimes rajas, or beans.

Although burritos are not usually found outside the northern areas of Mexico, their popularity exploded over the border and they became extremely popular in the United States. They are slowly growing in popularity in the central and southern regions of Mexico as well.

In this recipe hearty refried beans are topped with melted cheese and wrapped in a large flour tortilla. *Yield: Serves 4*

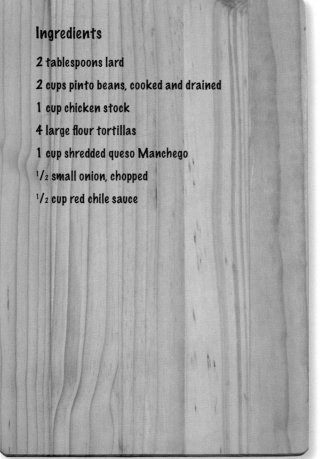

Ingredients

2 tablespoons lard

2 cups pinto beans, cooked and drained

1 cup chicken stock

4 large flour tortillas

1 cup shredded queso Manchego

1/2 small onion, chopped

1/2 cup red chile sauce

Bean and Cheese Burrito

- Melt the lard in a large saucepan over medium-high heat. Add the beans and mash.

- Add the chicken stock and let it simmer about 15 minutes, until the beans are thickened and creamy.

- Place beans on each tortilla and top with the cheese, onions, and chile sauce.

- Fold the burritos and place on a baking sheet; bake 5 minutes at 300°F.

Black Bean and Cheese: Substitute 2 cups of cooked or canned black bean for the pinto beans. Mash the beans as indicated in the recipe. You may also choose to leave them whole.

Pinto Bean and Cheese: If you want to forgo the mashing and frying part, substitute whole pinto beans, cooked or canned. If the beans are in a lot of liquid, drain some off before using so the tortilla doesn't get soggy. Don't rinse them or drain off too much liquid, though, as the bean broth has a lot of flavor to it.

Simmering the Beans

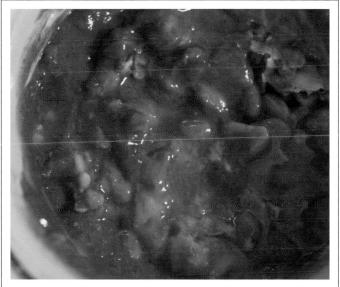

- Carefully add the chicken stock to the hot pan to avoid splatters.

- Simmer over very low heat, as refried beans have a tendency to burn or stick to the bottom of the pot if they are cooked over high heat.

- You want the beans to be the consistency of chunky peanut butter: firm yet spreadable.

- If you make the burrito with soupy beans, the tortilla may become soggy.

Rolling the Burritos

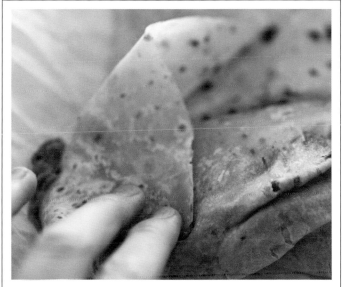

- Heat each tortilla on a hot comal about 10 seconds on each side to make them more pliable.

- Place the beans and cheese down the center of the tortilla. Fold the first edge of the tortilla over the beans and cheese lengthwise.

- Then fold the top and bottom edges over the filling, leaving one edge open.

- Fold the remaining side over to create a seam, and turn the whole burrito over so the seam is held down by the weight of the burrito.

STEAK QUESADILLA AMERICANA
This quesadilla is a feast for the palate

True quesadillas in Mexico are actually raw corn tortillas topped, folded in half, and fried to a golden brown. In the United States a quesadilla means something entirely different. It is cheese, and sometimes other ingredients such as meat or grilled vegetables, melted between two flour tortillas. In Mexico this dish of fillings sandwiched between two tortillas is known as a sincronizada.

No matter what you call them, this dish is delicious and easy to make. It can be featured as a main dish or served as an appetizer. It is also a great way to use leftovers, since just a small amount of meat, vegetables, or chiles goes a long way in a quesadilla. *Yield: Serves 2*

Ingredients

14-ounce top sirloin steak

¼ teaspoon salt

¼ teaspoon black pepper

1 lime, juiced

1 tablespoon oil

1 small red bell pepper

1 small green bell pepper

1 small white onion

½ teaspoon cumin

1 teaspoon ground chile

4 large flour tortillas

2 cups shredded Monterrey Jack cheese, divided

¼ cup red chile sauce

Steak Quesadilla Americana

- Coat the steak with salt, pepper, and lime juice; grill over medium-high heat until only slightly pink inside. Let it cool slightly; slice into ¼-inch pieces.

- Heat the oil in a saucepan over medium heat and sauté peppers, onion, and seasonings until softened.

- Heat a tortilla on a comal over low heat. Add ½ cup cheese, half the steak, half the pepper mixture, and top with remaining cheese and another tortilla. Heat until cheese is melted. Repeat with remaining ingredients. Add sauce and serve.

• • • • RECIPE VARIATIONS • • • •

Grilled Chicken Quesadilla Americana: Marinate about 14 ounces of boneless, skinless chicken in a basic marinade of salt, pepper, a drizzle of olive oil, and lime juice 30 minutes in the refrigerator. Grill over medium heat until cooked through. Slice and use it in place of the steak. You can even warm the quesadillas on the grill.

Vegetarian Quesadillas Americana: Gather together 2 cups of your favorite vegetables, such as sliced yellow squash, zucchini, onion, and bell pepper. Grilled portabella caps, sliced into strips, also make a delicious addition. Sauté the vegetables in 1 teaspoon cooking oil over medium heat until they are slightly softened. Use them in place of the steak.

Assembling the Quesadilla

- Heat a comal over low heat 1 or 2 minutes.

- Place a tortilla on the comal and heat it 10 seconds. Flip it over so the hot side is up, which will help the cheese melt faster.

- If you have a large comal, heat the other tortilla briefly before placing it on top, as the warmth will further help melt the cheese.

- Make sure the heat is low enough so the tortilla doesn't overcook while the cheese melts.

Cooking the Quesadilla

- Slide a large spatula under the quesadilla and use your fingers to help keep the top one in place.

- Quickly but carefully flip the quesadilla over so the fillings don't slide out.

- If the cheese is pretty much melted at this point, it will be much easier to flip.

- If any cheese does fall out, scrape it off the comal quickly or it may burn.

197

GRILLED CARNITAS BURRITO
Tender carnitas and zesty Mexican rice are a perfect match in this hearty burrito

Carnitas, meaning "little meats" in Spanish, are a very popular way to prepare pork in Mexico. Pork is simmered until fork–tender, and then it is fried in a bath of its own fat rendered off during the cooking process. The resulting pork is tender with bits of crispness from the frying.

While freshly made carnitas are the best choice, you can use leftover carnitas from last night's meal. Just reheat and use them where fresh carnitas are called for. Mexican Rice adds the delicious flavor of tomatoes, and the Crema Agria adds tanginess.

These burritos make a delicious and filling dinner, as well as a perfect portable lunch if you're on the go. *Yield: Serves 4*

Ingredients

¹/₂ cup Crema Agria

2 tablespoons heavy cream

2 garlic cloves, crushed

¹/₂ teaspoon salt

4 large flour tortillas

2 cups Mexican Rice

1 pound fresh carnitas

¹/₂ small onion, chopped

1 cup cilantro leaves

Grilled Carnitas Burrito

- Whisk together the Crema Agria, heavy cream, garlic, and salt in a mixing bowl until well combined.

- Warm tortillas on a comal 10 seconds each side.

- Place a quarter of the Mexican Rice, carnitas, onion, and cilantro down the cen-ter of each tortilla. Drizzle the cream sauce over the fillings.

- Wrap the tortilla around the fillings and grill on a medium-hot comal each side until tortilla browns and becomes crispy.

ZOOM

Substitutions: If you don't have any Crema Agria you can use sour cream instead. It has a similar flavor and texture. You can also substitute ¼ teaspoon garlic powder for the fresh garlic.

Serving Suggestions: To make it a meal, serve the burrito alongside a generous portion of black beans topped with spicy salsa. The smoky flavor of the beans compliments the combination of flavors in the burrito. You can also dip the burrito into the beans as you are eating it.

Assembling the Burrito

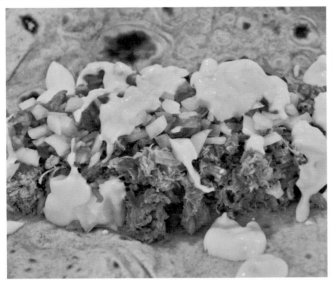

- Toast each tortilla on a comal just until warmed through.

- Place the toppings down the center of the tortilla, leaving 3 inches of space at one end.

- Fold one edge over the fillings lengthwise, then fold the bottom and top edges over.

- Fold the final edge over lengthwise to create a package. Flip the burrito over and let it rest for a moment to help mold the tortilla closed.

Grilling the Burrito

- Heat a comal over medium heat.

- Place the burrito, seam side down, onto the hot comal. Use a spatula to lightly press it down to ensure the surface of the burrito is browned evenly.

- Flip the burrito over and repeat on the other side until the burrito is golden and slightly crispy on the outside.

- Serve immediately.

BLACK BEAN & CHICKEN BURRITO
This hearty burrito is filled with grilled chicken, black beans, and avocado slices

In southern Mexico if you order beans in a restaurant, you will most likely be given black beans. They are the most popular type of bean consumed in that region. Chicken is another common ingredient in southern Mexican cuisine, and the mild flavors of cooked chicken breast are a delicious match for earthy black beans.

The addition of fresh salsa makes this burrito zesty and refreshing. Choose a salsa that is made with the freshest tomatoes, chile, and onions you can find.

Avocadoes, which are native to Mexico and have a creamy texture and unique flavor, make the perfect final touch to this hearty and satisfying burrito. *Yield: Serves 4*

Ingredients

¹/₂ teaspoon salt

¹/₂ teaspoon ground black pepper

3 boneless, skinless chicken breasts

4 large flour tortillas

1 cup cooked long-grain white rice

1 cup cooked and drained black beans

¹/₂ cup fresh salsa

1 avocado, cut into 8 slices

4 teaspoons hot chile sauce

1 cup cilantro leaves

Black Bean and Chicken Burrito

- Sprinkle the salt and pepper over the chicken breasts and grill over medium heat until cooked through. Cut the chicken into bite-size pieces.

- Warm a tortilla on a comal over medium heat until it begins to puff up slightly.

- Place one quarter of the rice, beans, chicken, and salsa and 2 slices avocado down the center of the tortilla. Fold the tortilla around the fillings; repeat with remaining ingredients and serve immediately with chile sauce and cilantro.

Using Leftover Chicken: A chicken burrito is the perfect use for leftovers. Reheat the chicken in a pan, cut it into bite-size pieces or shred it, and then use as directed in the burrito. Avoid using chicken that has strong seasonings that don't go well with Mexican flavors, such as rosemary, basil, or thyme.

Tomatoes and Crema Agria: Substitute the white rice with 1 cup freshly chopped tomatoes. Add 2 heaping tablespoons Crema Agria to each burrito before you roll it up.

Preparing the Chicken

- Cook the chicken until it is 170°F and no longer pink inside.

- Let the chicken rest 2 minutes before cutting it to allow it to redistribute the juices.

- Use a sharp knife to cut the chicken while holding it down with a fork.

- Have all the ingredients ready to assemble as soon as the chicken is ready so the chicken doesn't get cold.

Preparing the Burrito

- Warm tortillas are soft and pliable, so you will need to warm each one on a comal to soften it up.

- Place the ingredients down the center of each tortilla.

- Wrap each edge of the tortilla over the filling, starting with the lengthwise edge first.

- Follow by folding the edges at each end of the toppings and then finishing with the final lengthwise edge to seal the fillings inside.

SHRIMP BURRITO

Reminiscent of seaside fare, this burrito is full of succulent shrimp

In Mazatlan, which has the largest shrimp fleet in the world, the fishermen leave before dawn in their rustic boats to get the catch of the day. The seafood is abundant along the tropical coasts, and you will find various fish and shrimp dishes on just about every menu. The shrimp are large and succulent, perfect for a variety of shrimp dishes.

Shrimp Burritos are a perfect way to highlight the rich seafood flavors of fresh shrimp. The shrimp are cooked in a mixture of rice and traditional seasonings and then topped with a delicious creamy garlic sauce that is the perfect complement to the rich flavors of this burrito. *Yield: Serves 4*

Ingredients

1 tablespoon oil

2 cups cooked long-grain white rice

1/2 cup red chile sauce

Pinch ground cumin

1 garlic clove, crushed

1 teaspoon tomato paste

1/2 teaspoon salt

3 cups cooked shrimp, shells and tails removed

Garlic Cream Sauce

4 large flour tortillas

Shrimp Burrito

- In a large saucepan, heat the oil over medium heat. Add rice, chile sauce, cumin, garlic, tomato paste, and salt. Stir until combined.

- Reduce heat to low, add the shrimp, and continue to cook over low heat 2 minutes.

- Warm a tortilla on a comal over medium heat 10 seconds to make it pliable.

- Place one quarter shrimp mixture on the tortilla and top with Garlic Cream Sauce. Fold tortilla around filling; repeat with other tortillas and ingredients. Serve immediately.

•••• RECIPE VARIATION ••••

Garlic Cream Sauce: In a small saucepan, whisk together $1/2$ cup Crema Agria, $1/4$ cup heavy cream, and 2 tablespoons milk over low heat. Add 2 garlic cloves, chopped, along with $1/4$ teaspoon onion powder and $1/4$ teaspoon salt. Let the sauce cook over low heat 5 minutes to let the flavors meld.

Cooking the Rice

- Since the rice is already cooked, you only need to warm it and incorporate it with the other ingredients.

- Stir it often so that it warms quickly and evenly.

- Add the shrimp last so they don't become rubbery from being overcooked.

- Keep the heat extremely low so that the mixture does not burn or stick to the pan.

Filling the Burrito

- Place the filling down the center of a warm tortilla, but leave space at either end.

- Drizzle the Garlic Cream Sauce over the filling. You want enough to give it a good coating, but you don't want the filling swimming in it.

- Fold one of the lengthwise edges over the filling, followed by the edges at either end of the burrito.

- Fold the final edge over to keep the filling inside; let it rest momentarily, seam side down, before serving.

AGUA FRESCA

Make this refreshing and sweet beverage with your favorite fresh fruit

Agua fresca is term that encompasses many flavored sweet beverages, but it usually refers to fruit blended with water and sweetened to make a refreshing cool drink. The best part about agua fresca is that you can use any fruit that is in season; and even if the fruit is not sweet enough to your taste, you can add as much sugar as you like.

Agua fresca is also known as agua de fruta and is served by street vendors who ladle it by the cupful from large plastic barrels. It can also be flavored with the liquid from steeping hibiscus petals or with the pulp of tamarind pods. *Yield: Serves 6–8*

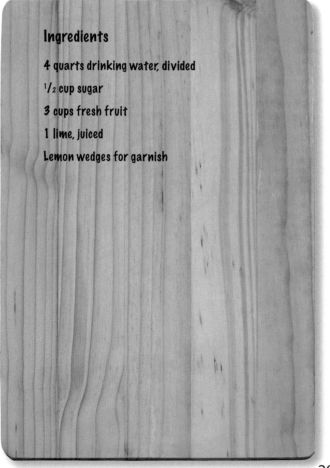

Ingredients

4 quarts drinking water, divided

$1/2$ cup sugar

3 cups fresh fruit

1 lime, juiced

Lemon wedges for garnish

Agua Fresca

- In a small saucepan heat 1 quart water and the sugar over medium heat. Simmer until the sugar is dissolved; let it cool.

- Place the fruit in a blender and cover with 2 quarts water. Puree until smooth.

- Pour the mixture through a sieve into a large pitcher.

- Add the remaining quart water, sugar mixture, and lime juice to the pitcher and stir until combined. Serve chilled with lemon wedges.

Agua de Jamaica Hibiscus: Bring 3 cups water to a boil and pour it over 2 ounces dried Jamaica hibiscus and ½ cup sugar. Let them soak 20 minutes and then strain out the liquid. Stir in an additional 4 cups ice-cold water and 1 cup ice.

Agua de Tamarindo: Heat 4 quarts water over high heat. Add ½ cup granulated sugar and bring to a boil; cook until sugar is dissolved. Remove from heat and stir in ¼ cup canned tamarind pulp. Let the mixture cool and then pour it into a pitcher and store in the refrigerator.

Blending the Fruit

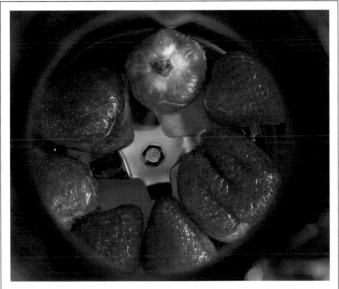

Assembling the Agua Fresca

BEVERAGES

- Prepare the fruit by removing stems and seeds as necessary. Cut larger fruits into smaller chunks and firm fruits into bite-size pieces.

- The water needs to cover the fruit by at least 2 inches to ensure even blending with no chunks.

- Stir the blended mixture, and if you feel any remaining chunks, continue to blend with the pulse feature until there are no lumps left.

- Place a sieve over a large pitcher and pour the pureed fruit mixture through it to sift out any remaining chunks.

- If the mixture begins to clog the sieve, use the back of a spoon to help press the fruit through.

- Depending on the fruit you use, there may be fibrous bits or seeds that may slow the liquid down as you pour it through. Use a spoon to scrape them out and discard.

ATOLE

This rich and thick masa porridge–like beverage will warm and soothe you on a chilly day

Atole is a traditional beverage that originates from the native Mayans, who often used masa to create porridge-like drinks. It is typically made with masa or masa harina and sweetened with a Mexican sugar called piloncillo.

Atole is usually served as a breakfast beverage and can range in consistency from a thin liquid to a thickened gruel.

Consumption of atole increases around the holiday season, when it is enjoyed as a traditional part of the celebrations and festivities. It is flavored with cinnamon and topped with a drizzle of pureed fruit that complements the richness of the atole. *Yield: Serves 4*

Ingredients

¹/₃ cup masa harina

1 cup warm water

3 cups water

4 ounces piloncillo, chopped

Pinch salt

¹/₄ teaspoon ground cinnamon

2 teaspoons vanilla

¹/₂ cup pureed strawberries

Atole

- Add the masa harina and warm water to a blender and pulse on low until well combined.

- Heat the 3 cups water in a medium pot until simmering. Slowly stir in the masa mixture and whisk to avoid clumping.

- Add the piloncillo, salt, cinnamon, and vanilla and simmer over the lowest heat setting 20 minutes, until the Atole begins to thicken.

- Serve Atole in mugs and add a couple of spoonfuls of pureed fruit to the top of each serving.

Strawberry Puree: Place 1 cup strawberries, 1 teaspoon sugar, and 2 tablespoons water into a blender. Pulse until ingredients are blended. If mixture is too thick, add water by the tablespoon until it is the desired consistency. If the strawberries are ripe and sweet, you might not need the sugar.

ZOOM

Fresh masa is corn that has been treated to remove the hulls and then ground into a soft dough. It is similar to reconstituted masa harina but has a slightly fresher taste. You will still need to blend the fresh masa with some water to make it easier to whisk into the larger amount of water.

BEVERAGES

Simmering the Atole

- Simmer the Atole slowly over the lowest heat setting to avoid scorching.

- Use a serrated knife to coarsely chop the piloncillo before adding it to the simmering masa mixture.

- If the liquid is cooking off too fast, add hot water to the pot ¼ cup at a time so that it has time to simmer the whole cooking time.

- If it is not thickening quickly enough, turn up the heat a little and stir continuously.

Serving the Atole

- The Atole is ready when it has slightly thickened. It will be slightly thicker than hot chocolate, but not as thick as a porridge.

- Top the Atole with a dollop or a drizzle of the puree. It can remain on top as a decoration or you can stir it in to get fruit flavor in each sip.

- The Atole will be very hot, so take care to let it cool so you don't scorch your mouth.

CHAMPURRADO

This rich chocolate drink is made with Mexican chocolate and flavored with anise

Champurrado is a hot chocolate beverage whisked with a tool called a molinillo until it becomes frothy. It has a slightly thickened consistency because it is cooked with masa harina.

Champurrado is often served with breakfast or enjoyed in the afternoon between meals. It is very popular during the winter holidays as well as for Día de Los Muertos, a holiday to celebrate the lives of the deceased.

This delicious beverage must be made with Mexican chocolate to give it a rich and authentic flavor.

The addition of anise seed adds a unique taste that is very common in Mexican cooking and provides a distinctive flavor.
Yield: Serves 4

Ingredients

¼ cup masa harina

2 cups warm water

1 disk Mexican chocolate

2 cups milk

4 ounces piloncillo

Pinch anise seed

Champurrado

- In a large pot, slowly whisk the masa harina into the warm water until thoroughly combined.

- Coarsely chop the chocolate with a serrated knife.

- Heat the water over low heat until it comes to a simmer. Add milk, chocolate, piloncillo, and anise.

- Continue to simmer 15 minutes, until the liquid begins to thicken slightly.

- Ladle the Champurrado into mugs and use a molinillo to create a froth on the top.

Mexican chocolate has a distinct taste because it is flavored with cinnamon and sometimes other spices. It has a somewhat grainy texture and is usually used for cooking and making chocolate drinks.

In the days of the Mayans and Aztecs, chocolate was a bitter beverage made with cocoa and chiles. While chocolate has become a sweet beverage, the addition of chile is still common. You can get the same spicy flavor by cooking the chocolate with a few strips of fresh jalapeño. Remove the jalapeño before serving.

Whisking the Masa and Water

- Pour the warm water into a large pot. Sprinkle a spoonful of the masa over the water and whisk it until it's completely incorporated. Repeat by the spoonful until all the masa has been whisked into the water.

- If any clumps develop, sift them out or use a spoon to remove them.

- The mixture should look like cloudy water when all the masa is incorporated.

Adding Froth

- The key to an authentic champurrado is making sure it is nice and frothy.

- Create a froth by using a molinillo to whip the champurrado and create a foamy head.

- Quickly roll the stem of the molinillo between your palms in a back-and-forth motion.

- When enough of the froth has formed, serve the Champurrado immediately.

MARGARITA

This tangy and refreshing cocktail features premium tequila and triple sec

Margaritas are a popular tequila-based beverage in Mexico and one of the most popular ways to enjoy a good tequila. Made with tangy lime juice and lightly sweetened with sugar and triple sec, they are easy to make and even easier to drink.

There are many stories surrounding the conception of this tasty drink. One of the most popular theories involves a lady named Margarita who lived in Mexico and set out to create a tequila cocktail. After years of mixing and perfecting her recipe, she came up with a drink that became the margarita.

Margaritas have since become the quintessential Mexican tequila drink that has come to represent the festive side of Mexico. *Yield: Serves 1*

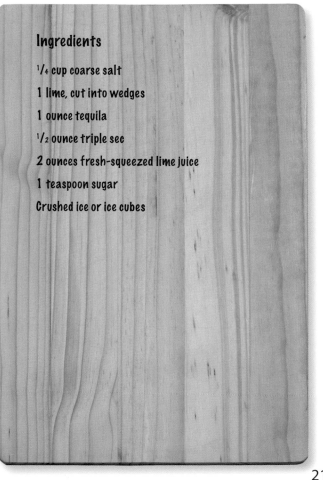

Ingredients

¼ cup coarse salt

1 lime, cut into wedges

1 ounce tequila

½ ounce triple sec

2 ounces fresh-squeezed lime juice

1 teaspoon sugar

Crushed ice or ice cubes

Margarita

- Pour the salt into a shallow dish. Rub a lime wedge around the rim of the glass and dip into the salt.

- In a shaker, combine the tequila, triple sec, lime juice, sugar, and ice. Place the lid on tightly and shake well to combine ingredients.

- Fill the salt-rimmed glass with ice and pour the margarita over.

- Serve immediately with additional lime wedges.

•••• RECIPE VARIATION ••••

Strawberry Margarita: To add the strawberries you will need to puree them first in a blender with a few tablespoons of water. Use 2 large or 3 small strawberries per drink. Use additional strawberries for garnish.

ZOOM

Triple sec is a type of alcohol made from dried curaçao orange peels. While most markets often carry a generic brand , name brands such as Curaçao, Cointreau, and Grand Marnier make premium versions. Cointreau is most often used, and there is a Cadillac margarita that features a shot of Grand Marnier floated on the top.

Preparing the Ingredients

Serving the Margarita

- Using a lime press to juice the limes is the best way to get the most juice possible with very little effort.

- Large, juicy limes are the key to creating a delicious margarita. Look for limes that have a thin, tight skin and are heavy for their size.

- Use a cocktail jigger to make sure the perfect amount of each ingredient goes into each margarita.

- Salt around the rim of the glass is the signature margarita garnish. Rub a lime wedge around the rim of the glass and let it dry momentarily to create a sticky surface for the salt.

- Carefully add the ice to the glass so you don't knock too much of the salt off.

- Pour the drink over the ice, being careful not to wash off any of the salt.

- Garnish the rim of the glass with a lime wedge.

SANGRITA

This seasoned tomato drink is meant to be sipped alongside your favorite premium tequila

The origins of Sangrita lie in Jalisco, Mexico, where it was created to sip along with tequila. Sangrita was sipped to add flavor and also to refresh the palate between the sips of tequila.

In Mexico if you order your tequila *completo* you will get a serving of chilled sangrita with your tequila, as well as a lime wedge to squeeze into the sangrita.

Sangrita combines spicy chile with tangy tomato and the sweetness of orange juice with the bite of salt. It is a small example of the types of contrasting flavors Mexicans enjoy in their food and drink.

There are a few commercially made Sangritas, but it is so much more flavorful when you make it yourself. *Yield: Serves 4*

Ingredients

³/₄ cup tomato sauce

¹/₂ cup orange juice

3 limes

¹/₄ teaspoon onion powder

¹/₄ teaspoon salt

¹/₂ teaspoon sugar

¹/₂ teaspoon chile powder

2 tablespoons hot chile sauce

8 ounces premium tequila

Sangrita

- Place all the ingredients except the tequila in a blender and pulse on high speed until thoroughly combined.

- Pour the blended mixture into a shaker with ice, place the top on securely, and shake vigorously to chill.

- Pour the Sangrita into a small tumbler or large shot glass and serve it next to a 2 oz. shot of premium tequila.

Vampiro: Sangrita is usually served alongside tequila. And they are sipped one at a time. Vampiro is a beverage made with tequila and sangrita together. In a small tumbler mix together 1 ounce tequila, 1 ounce lime juice, and 3 ounces sangrita; top if off with 1 or 2 ounces club soda. Garnish with a few lime wedges and enjoy.

Michelada: Empty a cold Mexican beer into a frosty salt-rimmed beer mug, leaving some room for other ingredients. Stir in 1 ounce sangrita, the juice of 1 lime, 2 dashes hot chile sauce, and 1 dash maggi sauce. Maggi sauce is a Swedish sauce that is similar to soy sauce and is popular in Mexico. Add more beer as you drink the cocktail.

Blending the Ingredients

- Due to their dry texture, it is necessary to blend the powdered spices into the liquids so they don't clump up.

- If you do not have a blender, mix a spoonful of the liquid into the powdered spices to form a thick paste. Add an additional spoonful of liquid to thin it out further and then whisk the thin paste into the remaining tomato mixture.

Serving the Sangrita

- Use high-quality ingredients for the best results.

- You can make the Sangrita up to 24 hours in advance and keep it chilled in the refrigerator until you are ready to serve it.

- If you are serving it from the refrigerator, you don't have to shake it with ice to chill it.

- Premium tequilas are meant to be sipped and enjoyed, so select a top-of-the-line tequila to pair with your Sangrita.

ROMPOPE

Enjoy this delicious eggnog-style holiday beverage flavored with almonds, cinnamon, and rum

Rompope is a popular holiday beverage that is thought to originate from the state of Puebla, where nuns made it over two thousand years ago. Egg-based beverages were common in Spain, and when the Spanish conquistadors began settling into Mexico, they brought their culinary influences with them.

Rompope is traditionally made with rum, but there are other versions that use other spirits such as whisky or bourbon. Rompope can also be used as an ingredient in other recipes for cakes and other desserts.

While rum adds a signature flavor, it can be left out if a non-alcoholic version is desired. Add a splash of vanilla instead. *Yield: Serves 6–8*

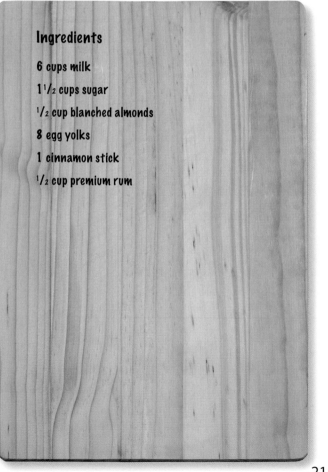

Ingredients

6 cups milk

1 1/2 cups sugar

1/2 cup blanched almonds

8 egg yolks

1 cinnamon stick

1/2 cup premium rum

Rompope

- In a large pot bring the milk and sugar to a simmer over low heat.

- Process the almonds in a food processor until a paste forms. A spoonful at a time, add the milk mixture to the paste. Then combine the paste with the remaining milk mixture.

- Beat the egg yolks until creamy. Slowly pour the eggs into the milk mixture while stirring. Stir in the rum and serve chilled.

•••• RECIPE VARIATION ••••

Blanched Almonds: Blanched almonds are almonds that have had their dark brown skins removed and only the whitish flesh remains. To make them, boil 3 cups water in a medium saucepan. Add the almonds to the boiling water and cook 1 minute. Remove them from the boiling water and rinse under cold water 1 minute. Pat them dry and then rub the skins off.

ZOOM

Rum has a warm, rich flavor. It is the by-product of manufacturing molasses, or it is distilled from sugar cane. Rum aged in steel tanks is clear, while rum that has been aged in oak develops a golden tone (as it continues to age it becomes a deeper brown). Spiced rum is flavored with cinnamon and can be used to make rompope.

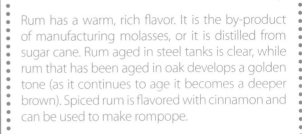

BEVERAGES

Almond Paste

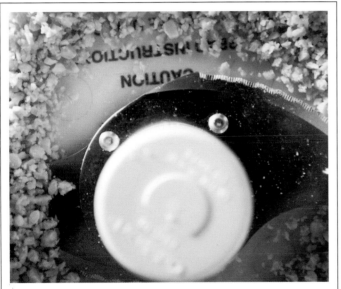

- Place the blanched almonds into a food processor all at once.

- Pulse the almonds on low speed until they are ground up and have formed a paste similar to peanut butter.

- Use a rubber spatula to scrape the sides and ensure all the almonds are removed.

- If a food processor is not available, crush the almonds with ½ cup milk until they are completely ground.

Blending the Ingredients

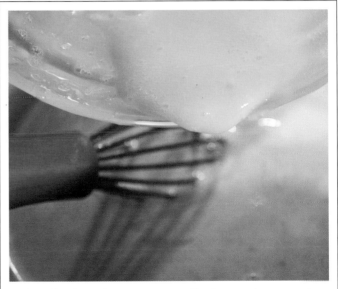

- Place the almond paste into a large mixing bowl, add 1 tablespoon milk mixture, and stir it in.

- Continue to add milk mixture 1 tablespoon at a time until the almond paste is watered down.

- Slowly pour the watered-down paste into the remaining milk mixture and stir together until it is well combined.

PASTEL DE TRES LECHES

This is a moist and creamy cake topped with whipped cream and fresh berries

The use of three different types of milk is what gives this delicious and moist cake its name. The milks are evaporated milk, sweetened condensed milk, and heavy cream. After soaking in the sweetened milk mixture, the cake is topped with freshly whipped cream and usually garnished with berries.

The use of condensed milk became popular in the 1800s, when sugar was used to help preserve canned milk. Soon after, evaporated milk was introduced. Both were shelf stable and made great milk substitutes when fresh milk was not available. These canned milks became popular in Central America as well as in Mexico, where the use of refrigeration was limited. *Yield: Serves 8–10*

Ingredients

1¹/₂ cups cake flour

1 teaspoon baking powder

¹/₄ teaspoon salt

¹/₃ cup oil

1 cup sugar

1 teaspoon vanilla extract

5 extra-large eggs

1 cup milk

Leche Sauce

1 cup heavy cream whipped with 1 tablespoon sugar

30 fresh berries for garnish

Pastel de Tres Leches

- Combine flour, baking powder, and salt in a large bowl.

- In a separate bowl, mix oil, sugar, vanilla, and eggs. Stir in milk; fold in flour mixture a little at a time until well combined.

- Pour batter into a greased

9x13 inch pan; bake at 325°F 35 minutes.

- Let cake cool and turn it over onto a platter with raised edges. Pierce with a fork 20 to 30 times and pour Leche Sauce over it. Refrigerate 1 hour; frost with whipped cream and garnish with berries.

Leche Sauce: Whisk together 1 teaspoon vanilla extract, 2 5-ounce cans evaporated milk, 1 12-ounce can sweetened condensed milk, ½ cup heavy cream, 1 tablespoon rum, and a pinch of salt. Refrigerate mixture to chill. You can make the sauce up to 24 hours in advance. If the sauce separates, rewhisk it before using.

Adding Leche Sauce

- Slowly pour Leche Sauce over the cooled cake so it has time to absorb while you pour.

- Refrigerate a minimum of 1 hour and as long as 3.

- Occasionally, spoon the milk runoff back onto the cake.

- There will be additional liquid that is not absorbed into the cake, which is fine.

Frosting the Cake

- Chill a mixing bowl in the refrigerator 30 minutes to keep the cream cool.

- In a mixer beat the cream and sugar on high speed until stiff peaks form.

- Whipped cream will hold in the refrigerator up to 24 hours if you need to make it ahead of time.

- Spoon the excess liquid from the cake onto each plate before serving a slice.

MEXICAN WEDDING CAKES

A light and airy cookie flavored with roasted pecans that melts in your mouth

Mexican wedding cakes are crispy cookies with a lovely combination of sweet and salty. While the salt in the sugar coating is almost imperceptible, it gives these delicious cookies their signature flavor. The use of butter, sugar, and flour without any eggs gives Mexican wedding cakes their velvety, yet crumbly texture.

These cookies are also known as Russian tea cakes and polvorones, but the recipes are all similar, made from flour, sugar, and roasted pecans and then rolled in powdered sugar. Mexican wedding cakes are popular during the winter holidays, but they are also well suited as a summertime treat because of their light and airy texture. *Yield: Serves 16*

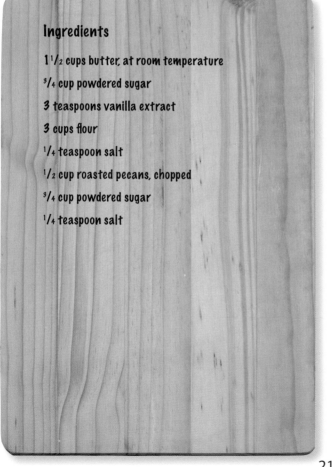

Ingredients

1½ cups butter, at room temperature

¾ cup powdered sugar

3 teaspoons vanilla extract

3 cups flour

¼ teaspoon salt

½ cup roasted pecans, chopped

¾ cup powdered sugar

¼ teaspoon salt

Mexican Wedding Cakes

- Mix butter, ¾ cup powdered sugar, and vanilla in a mixer until combined.

- In a separate bowl, mix flour and ¼ teaspoon salt. Mix the flour into the butter mixture about ½ cup at a time until well incorporated. Carefully fold in the pecans.

- Roll the dough into balls about 1 tablespoon each and place on an ungreased baking sheet.

- Bake at 350°F about 15 minutes. Mix ¾ cup powdered sugar and ¼ teaspoon salt. Roll the warm cookies in the sugar mixture.

Roasted Pecans: Preheat the oven to 350°F. Arrange pecans in a single layer on a baking sheet. Bake 8 to 10 minutes, until they become golden brown and toasted.

Using Other Nuts: You can substitute other nuts if pecans are not available or you want a different flavor. Hazelnuts make a good choice, because they are similar to pecans in texture. Walnuts can also be used, as can a combination of any of the above. Whichever nuts you choose, roast them in the same manner as the pecans.

Preparing the Cookies

- The dough has plenty of butter in it, so you do not need to grease the baking sheet.

- The dough will not spread out, so you can place the cookies fairly close together. Leave at least

- 1 inch of space between them so the hot air can circulate to cook them evenly.

- Make sure the oven has reached 350°F before you bake the cookies or they may not become crispy.

Coating the Cookies

- Let the cookies cool briefly before you roll them or you might burn your fingers.

- Do not let them cool completely, however, or the sugar coating will not stick.

- Place the sugar mixture in a shallow dish so there is plenty of room to roll the cookies around.

- Pick up a cookie, place it in the sugar mixture, and lightly roll it around until it is completely coated. You can roll the cookies a second time after they cool.

DESSERTS

ARROZ CON LECHE

Enjoy this sweet and creamy rice pudding for breakfast or as a snack

This tasty rice dish makes a delicious dessert and can also be enjoyed for breakfast or a snack. The concept for arroz con leche was introduced into Mexico by the invading Spanish conquistadors, who began to import many of their own European ingredients and recipes to the New World. Arroz con Leche was no exception, and soon the sweet rice dish that was enjoyed by the Spanish became popular in Mexico.

Rice, milk, and sugar are always the main ingredients for Arroz con Leche no matter which Latin country you find it in, but the other additions such as raisins, lime or lemon peel, cinnamon or vanilla vary from country to country. *Yield: Serves 4–6*

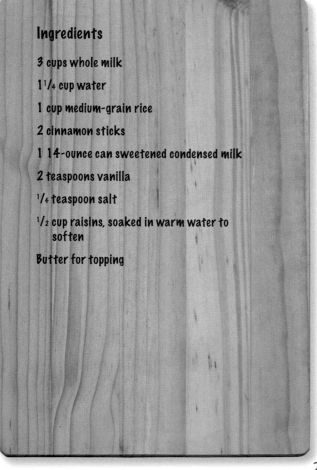

Ingredients

3 cups whole milk

1¼ cup water

1 cup medium-grain rice

2 cinnamon sticks

1 14-ounce can sweetened condensed milk

2 teaspoons vanilla

¼ teaspoon salt

½ cup raisins, soaked in warm water to soften

Butter for topping

Arroz con Leche

- In a medium pot bring whole milk and water to a slow simmer over medium-low heat.

- Stir in rice and cinnamon sticks and simmer uncovered about 30 minutes, until rice is softened, stirring occasionally.

- When rice is soft, remove cinnamon sticks and stir in condensed milk, vanilla, salt, and raisins. Return to a simmer and cook an additional 10 to 15 minutes, until most of the liquid is absorbed and rice has a pudding-like consistency.

Long-Grain Rice: Medium-grain rice is great for Arroz con Leche because of its sticky, creamy texture. If you prefer a fluffier rice pudding with the grains of rice more evident, you can use long-grain rice. The cooking method will be the same as for medium-grain rice, but the final result will not be as glutenous and creamy.

Lime Arroz con Leche: To add a little lime flavor, squeeze a lime wedge or two over the top and stir in the juice. For a stronger lime flavor, add 1 teaspoon finely grated lime zest into the rice mixture while it is cooking. Garnish with additional lime wedges.

Simmering the Rice

- Simmer the rice slowly for a long time, stirring frequently.

- The key is that the liquid cooks off at the same time as the rice cooks, making a creamy consistency.

- If the liquid boils off too fast you will be left with uncooked rice. You can add water by the tablespoon to replace the liquid if it cooks off too fast.

Serving the Rice Pudding

- The Arroz con Leche can be served warm with a pat of butter on the top.

- Warm Arroz con Leche makes a great breakfast.

- Arroz con Leche can be refrigerated and served cold. It will have a thicker consistency, and no butter is added.

- Whether it is served warm or cold, a sprinkle of ground cinnamon over the top adds flavor.

DESSERTS

CAPIROTADA

Pecans, raisins, apples, and cheese add flavor and texture to this Mexican bread pudding

This rich and hearty sweet dish is made by toasting chunks of stale bread in butter until they are golden, then adding various fruits, nuts, and cheese and baking them together in a piloncillo syrup. An egg mixture is also added during baking, which gives the dish its pudding-like consistency. Spices such as cinnamon and cloves add a warm, earthy flavor that complements the other ingredients.

Like many dishes in Mexico, capirotada has Spanish influences stemming from the Spanish invasion of Mexico in the 1500s. It is often enjoyed during Lent, which is a religious tradition and involves giving up meat for a period of time. It is also consumed during the winter holidays. *Yield: Serves 8–10*

Ingredients

¼ cup butter

6 cups stale Mexican bread cut into large chunks

2 large or 3 small apples, peeled, cored, and chopped

²/₃ cup pecans, chopped

1 cup raisins soaked in warm water to soften

1 tablespoon orange zest

1 teaspoon lemon zest

½ cup crumbled queso fresco

½ teaspoon cloves

1 teaspoon cinnamon

Piloncillo Syrup

4 egg yolks

4 cups milk

Pinch salt

¼ cup sherry

Capirotada

- In a large saucepan, melt butter over medium heat. Fry the bread until golden.

- In a large bowl, combine the bread with the apples, pecans, raisins, zests, and cheese. Sprinkle cloves and cinnamon on top.

- Layer half the bread mixture, drizzled with half the syrup, in a buttered baking dish. Layer the remaining bread and syrup and bake 35 minutes at 350°F.

- Beat egg yolks with the milk, salt, and sherry. Pour over bread and bake 35 minutes, until top is golden.

Piloncillo Syrup: Heat 1¼ cups water in a small saucepan over high heat. Chop up 16 ounces piloncillo with a serrated knife. When the water begins to boil, add the piloncillo, 1 cinnamon stick, and 1 teaspoon anise seeds.

Turn the heat down so the liquid simmers gently. Let it cook down about 10 minutes, until the liquid becomes syrupy. Remove the cinnamon stick before using.

Frying the Bread

- Use a shallow pan to heat the butter over medium heat. It is ready when the butter foams up slightly.

- Place enough bread in the hot butter so that it fills the pan, yet there is still room to move them around.

- Turn each piece so each side becomes golden. Drain the pieces on paper towels and begin to fry the next batch.

- Adjust heat as necessary to keep it steady and to avoid burning the bread.

Adding the Egg Mixture

- Remove the baking dish from the oven and let it cool a few minutes.

- Put the egg mixture into a pitcher or something meant for pouring.

- Pour the egg mixture over the bread quickly to avoid curdling the eggs.

- Pour it over the bread so it is evenly distributed.

DESSERTS

FLAN

A rich caramel sauce smothers this traditional custard of milk and eggs

Flan is one of the most popular dessert dishes in Mexican cuisine and can be found on almost every restaurant menu. It is also commercially made. Sweets were largely unknown in Mexico until the sixteenth century, when the Spaniards first introduced sugar and other foods as they were trying to take over the land.

Mexicans incorporated the new ingredients and techniques into their own native cuisine, and sweet dishes flourished. Flan is a custard that is cooked in a water bath to avoid curdling. It is baked in small dishes lined with caramel. After the flan is cooked and cooled, the dishes are turned over so that the caramel sauce coats the custard. *Yield: Serves 12*

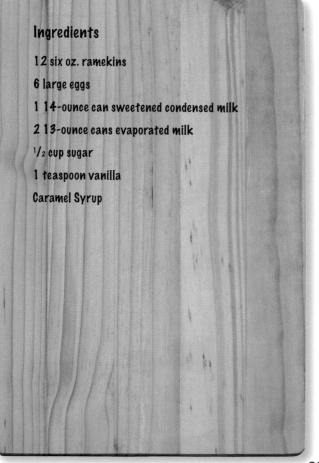

Ingredients

12 six oz. ramekins

6 large eggs

1 14-ounce can sweetened condensed milk

2 13-ounce cans evaporated milk

1/2 cup sugar

1 teaspoon vanilla

Caramel Syrup

Flan

- Pre-heat the oven to 325°F. With a mixer or whisk, blend the eggs together. Slowly mix in the condensed milk, evaporated milk, sugar, and vanilla.

- Pour approximately 2 to 3 tablespoons Caramel Syrup into each ramekin, tilting it to swirl the caramel around the sides.

- Pour the custard into the caramel-lined ramekins. Place ramekins into a water bath.

- Bake 45 minutes and let cool in the refrigerator 1 hour. Invert each ramekin onto a small plate; serve chilled.

Caramel Syrup: Pour 1 cup sugar into a warm pan over medium-low heat. Stir constantly until it begins to turn golden. Reduce heat to low and continue to stir until the sugar melts completely, turns a rich brown hue, and becomes caramel. Use the caramel while it is still warm, as once it cools down it will harden. If caramel begins to harden, simply reheat until it becomes liquid again.

ZOOM

If you don't want to make your own caramel syrup, substitute a jar of caramel syrup. It is found in the baking section of the grocery store, or it might be labeled as an ice-cream topping. Just heat it over low heat in a small saucepan and use it as driected.

Lining the Ramekins

- The Caramel Syrup hardens quickly, so keep it warm over the lowest possible heat setting and return it to the heat between preparing each ramekin.

- The Caramel Syrup should be swirled around to coat the sides of the ramekin,

but you can also put the Caramel Syrup on the bottom.

- It's okay if the Caramel Syrup thickens or hardens before you put the custard in, as it will soften during the cooking process.

Baking the Flan

- The water bath diffuses the heat and prevents the eggs from curdling.

- To create a water bath, you need a baking dish large enough to hold all the ramekins.

- Fill the baking dish with 1 inch warm water and place

the ramekins into the water; bake as directed.

- Be very careful with the water bath, as it will be very heavy.

DESSERTS

CALABAZA EN TACHA

Piloncillo, orange zest, and cinnamon are the keys to authentic and delicious candied pumpkin

Calabaza en Tacha is pumpkin that has been simmered in a piloncillo syrup until it is soft and tender. This sweet pumpkin dish is popular during the Mexican festivities of Día de los Muertos (Day of the Dead), which fall on the first two days of November.

Día de los Muertos is a celebration of the lives of those family and friends who have passed on, and Calabaza en Tacha is often placed on the *offrendas,* which are altars for loved ones, as sustenance for their long journey.

Pumpkins are harvested in the fall, which makes them a perfect ingredient for Día de los Muertos. *Yield: Serves 4–6*

Ingredients

5 pounds cooking pumpkin

2 pounds piloncillo, chopped

Juice of 1 orange

Zest of 1 orange

4 cinnamon sticks

4 cups water

Calabaza en Tacha

- Cut the stem off the pumpkin and cut the pumpkin in half. Scrape out the seeds and stringy parts. Cut each piece into strips and slice the skin off.

- Cut each strip into 2-inch pieces and place them in a large saucepan. Add the piloncillo, orange juice, orange zest, cinnamon sticks, and water and simmer uncovered over low heat 2 hours.

- Remove from heat, remove the cinnamon sticks, and let it cool to room temperature before serving.

If you don't have piloncillo, reproduce the rich flavor with 1¾ cup dark brown sugar and ¼ cup molasses. Another alternative is to use 2 cups raw sugar, which is minimally processed and still retains some of the molasses flavors similar to piloncillo.

• • • • RECIPE VARIATION • • • •

Pumpkin Skin: Some recipes call for the pumpkin skin to be left on. If you opt to leave the skin on, use a knife to score it in straight lines lengthwise at an angle and then cross them with horizontal lines to create a diamond pattern. Cook the pumpkin as directed.

Preparing the Pumpkin

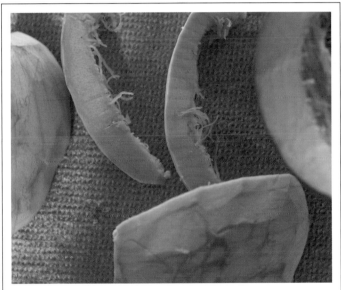

Cooking the Pumpkin

- Remove the seeds and stringy interior by scraping them out with a large metal spoon.

- Pumpkin flesh is very stringy, so even though you may feel as though you're scraping out the stringiness, you may actually be digging out flesh.

- Fresh pumpkin has a very hard flesh, so be sure to use a sharp knife to cut it into strips.

- Fresh pumpkin is also very slimy, so be careful not to slip. You can use a fork to hold the pumpkin in place while you cut it.

- Simmer the pumpkin in the syrup until the pumpkin is soft and fork-tender.

- Keep the heat on the lowest possible setting so the syrup doesn't scorch.

- The dish is ready when the liquid has cooked off and is reduced to a thick glaze.

- Calabaza en Tacha is typically served at room temperature, so let it cool before serving.

GEAR & INGREDIENTS

To create truly authentic Mexican dishes it is important to use traditional cooking equipment. Beans made in a stainless steel pot won't have quite the same flavor as beans cooked in a traditional Mexican bean pot called an olla. Think of the recipes you will be making most often, and get started with one or two key pieces and build up from there.

Where to find Mexican cooking equipment

Chef Latino
www.cheflatino.com

Gourmet Sleuth
www.gourmetsleuth.com/cItems.asp?i=15&c=6

IMUSA
www.imusausa.com/products/

Melissa Guerra
www.melissaguerra.com/list.cfm/ct/1

Mex Grocer
www.mexgrocer.com

Mi Fiesta
www.mifiesta.com/mexican-cookware.html

Where to find Mexican ingredients

Grocery Stores
With Mexican food growing in popularity you are likely to find a Hispanic section in most large chain stores. If you don't see what you need, talk to a manager to see if they can get you what you need.

Mexican Markets

Depending on your location, you may be able to find local Mexican specialty store to purchase items such as a carniceria for meats or a panaderia for bread.

Online Resources

You should be able to find just about everything you need online. The only drawback is that you can't see the item in person before ordering, and there are often shipping charges included. However, many stores offer shipping deals and have excellent return policies. Here are some great online resources.

Gourmet Sleuth
www.gourmetsleuth.com/subcat.asp?i=19

Local Farmers Market
www.localharvest.org/farmers-markets

Mex Grocer
www.mexgrocer.com

Mesa Mexican Foods
www.mesamexicanfoods.com/market/index.php

Mi Fiesta
www.mifiesta.com/mexican-food.html

The Spice House
www.thespicehouse.com/spices-by-cuisine/mexican-spices-and-seasonings

228

Mexican Ingredients

Here is a list of common ingredients you may want to keep on hand to create authentic Mexican cuisine whenever you want. Print it out and take it with you shopping. If you have a particular recipe in mind, check the ingredients needed to make sure you get everything necessary.

Dry Goods

Beef stock or broth
Black beans
Canned goods
Chicken stock or broth
Chipotle chiles in adobo sauce
Diced green chiles
Evaporated milk
Green chile sauce
Jalapeños
Other assorted chiles
Red chile sauce
Refried beans
Sweetened condensed milk
Tamarind (Tamarindo)
Tomato sauce
Whole green chiles

Chiles—dried, powdered, canned or paste

Anaheim
Ancho
Cascabel
Chile Negro
Chipotle
Guajillo
Hatch
Jalepeño
New Mexico
Pasilla
Poblano
Serrano

Dried Beans and/or Rice

Black beans
Pinto beans
White rice, long grain
White rice, medium grain

Seasonings— dried or ground

Achiote
Anise
Bay leaves
Cilantro
Cinnamon sticks
Cloves
Cumin
Epazote
Garlic powder
Hoja Santa
Onion powder
Oregano
Parsley
Saffron
Standard chile powder
Vanilla
Vanilla beans

Breads/Flours

Cornmeal
Corn tortillas
Flour tortillas
Hominy, frozen or dried
Masa Harina
White flour

Fresh/Refrigerated— produce:

Assorted green chiles
Assorted red chiles
Avocado
Bell pepper
Cilantro
Cucumber
Epazote
Garlic
Green onion
Jicama
Limes
Lemons
Onion
Parsley
Plantains
Potatoes
Tomatoes
Tomatillos

Cheese/Dairy:

Cotija
Crema
Jack
Panela
Queso Fresco
Queso Blanco
Queso Enchilado

Protein:

Chicken breasts
Chicken pieces
Chorizo
Eggs
Flank or skirt steak (for Carne Asada or Fajitas)
Ground beef
Lamb
Large beef cuts (for stews and roasts)
Pork loin
Pork roast
Ribs (beef or pork)
Veal
Whole chicken
Other:
  Chile sauce
  Coarse salt
  Honey
  Lard
  Mexican chocolate
  Piloncillo
  Sugar
  Tequila
  Tortilla chips
  Unsweetened chocolate
  Vegetable oil

ADDITIONAL COOKING REFERENCES

Online videos and printed cookbooks can teach you even more about cooking Mexican food. Learn new techniques by watching a video or two and try new recipes to discover more about this delicious cuisine.

How-to videos

About.com
http://video.about.com/food.htm

5min Food
www.5min.com/Category/Food/Latin

ifood
www.ifood.tv/network/mexican_food/recipes

Wonder How To
www.wonderhowto.com/search/mexican-food/food/

Mexican cookbooks

Authentic Mexican by Rick Bayless with Deann Groen
- A collection of authentic Mexican recipes from quick and easy to gourmet.

The Essential Cuisines of Mexico by Diana Kennedy
- Diana Kennedy's three best-selling cookbooks combined into one with over 300 recipes.

The Food and Life of Oaxaca by Zarela Martinez
- Take a closer look at the flavors of Oaxaca with recipes from and history of this colorful Mexican state.

Food from My Heart by Zarela Martinez
- A selection of recipes woven together with personal stories and Mexican history.

Jim Peyton's New Cooking from Old Mexico by Jim Peyton
- A collection of delicious recipes and highlights of the history of Mexican Cuisine.

Mexico, One Plate at a Time by Rick Bayless
- Features recipes that can be made in thirty minutes or less and takes a look at nutrition.

My Mexico by Diana Kennedy
- This cookbook features 300 recipes and an intimate look at the culture and cuisine of Mexico.

Rick Bayless's Mexican Kitchen by Rick Bayless
- This award-winning cookbook will impress you with 135 delicious regional recipes.

WEB SITES & BLOGS
Mexican food Web sites and blogs

RESOURCES

About.com Mexican
mexicanfood.about.com

Marcela Valladoid
www.chefmarcela.com

Gourmet Sleuth Mexican Recipes
www.gourmetsleuth.com/mexican_recipes.htm

Mex Grocer
http://mexican-supermarket.com

Lo Mexicano Recipes and History
http://lomexicano.com/

RickBayless
http://www.rickbayless.com/

METRIC CONVERSION TABLES
Approximate U.S. Metric Equivalents

Liquid Ingredients

U.S. MEASURES	METRIC	U.S. MEASURES	METRIC
¼ TSP.	1.23 ML	2 TBSP.	29.57 ML
½ TSP.	2.36 ML	3 TBSP.	44.36 ML
¾ TSP.	3.70 ML	¼ CUP	59.15 ML
1 TSP.	4.93 ML	½ CUP	118.30 ML
1¼ TSP.	6.16 ML	1 CUP	236.59 ML
1½ TSP.	7.39 ML	2 CUPS OR 1 PT.	473.18 ML
1¾ TSP.	8.63 ML	3 CUPS	709.77 ML
2 TSP.	9.86 ML	4 CUPS OR 1 QT.	946.36 ML
1 TBSP.	14.79 ML	4 QTS. OR 1 GAL.	3.79 L

Dry Ingredients

U.S. MEASURES	METRIC	U.S. MEASURES		METRIC
⅟₁₆ OZ.	2 (1.8) G	2⅘ OZ.		80 G
⅛ OZ.	3½ (3.5) G	3 OZ.		85 (84.9) G
¼ OZ.	7 (7.1) G	3½ OZ.		100 G
½ OZ.	15 (14.2) G	4 OZ.		115 (113.2) G
¾ OZ.	21 (21.3) G	4½ OZ.		125 G
⅞ OZ.	25 G	5¼ OZ.		150 G
1 OZ.	30 (28.3) G	8⅞ OZ.		250 G
1¾ OZ.	50 G	16 OZ.	1 LB.	454 G
2 OZ.	60 (56.6) G	17⅗ OZ.	1 LIVRE	500 G

MEXICAN HOLIDAY FARE

RESOURCES

Many Mexican dishes are prepared for certain holidays such as Day of the Dead and Las Posadas. Many times they represent the rich history and culture and are eaten as part of the holiday festivities to commemorate an event.

Día de los Muertos (Day of the Dead)

This holiday evolved when the Spaniards invaded Mexico and brought their Catholic beliefs with them. They tried to incorporate Catholic holidays and beliefs into the existing Aztec rituals and practices of worshiping the dead.

Día de los Muertos is a lively and colorful celebration of those who have passed on. It is not a morbid event, but a festive one to celebrate the lives that they led. Mexicans often construct altars draped with colorful oilcloth and fabric. They adorn the altars with pictures of the deceased as well as food and beverage to nourish the spirits that may visit. Flowers and personal items are often left on the altar as well.

Lightly sweet Pan de Muerto, or Bread of the Dead, is decorated with bone shapes and enjoyed as part of the festivities. Candied Pumpkin is another dish that is not only consumed, but can be placed on the altar as well.

Sugar is formed into skull shapes and decorated with brightly colored icing, colored foil, beads and feathers to create colorful folkloric pieces that are displayed on the altars and used as decorations.

For more information about Day of the Dead and Sugar Skull making supplies you can visit www.mexicansugarskull.com

Winter Holidays

While in many countries Christmas represents a single holiday to celebrate, in Mexico there are multiple celebrations over the course of the winter months. One of the main celebrations is Las Posadas which is a Catholic tradition brought over by the invading Spaniards. Las Posadas commemorates Joseph's and Mary's search for shelter with candlelight processions and traditional songs and ends with a feast or a party. The food served included tamales, ponche (fruit punch) and Atole. The celebrations begin on December 16th and continue for nine days and is followed by Navidad which is the Christmas celebration.

The festivities continue to Día de Los Santos Reyes on January 6th which is a celebration of the three wise men bringing gifts to Jesus. Gifts are exchanged and Rosca de Reyes (Three Kings Bread) is eaten as part of the celebrations.

Cinco de Mayo and Mexican Independence Day

Cinco de Mayo is not Mexico's Independence day as widely believed in the U.S. It is in fact a celebration of winning the battle of Puebla against the French and is not a major holiday in Mexico. The celebrations take place mainly in the city of Puebla itself. Cinco de Mayo outside of Mexico is a day to celebrate the culture and heritage of Mexico. Mexican food, such as tacos and burritos are enjoyed as part of the festivities.

Mexico's Independence day is on September 16th and commemorates the call to revolt against the Spanish. A dish called Chiles en Nogada is served throughout the country around this time. The colors of the dish (green chile, white sauce and red pomegranate seeds) represent the Mexican flag and are a reminder of the celebration of independence.

GLOSSARY

Achiote: A bright red paste made from annatto seeds, vinegar, lime juice, and seasonings. It is popular in the Yucatan area.

Adobo: A marinade and sauce made with chiles, onions, and vinegar. Chipotle chiles are often canned in this sauce.

Ancho: A poblano chile that has been dried. It's slightly sweet and has a raisin flavor.

Arroz Rice: It can mean uncooked rice or a finished rice dish.

Bolillo: A chewy roll with a golden, crispy exterior. Often used for Mexican tortas.

Camarón: Shrimp

Carne: Meat, usually beef

Chipotle: Ripe jalepeño, smoked and dried. Can be canned in Adobo sauce.

Chorizo: Heavily seasoned ground fresh sausage. Different from Spanish chorizo, which is dried.

Cilantro: Fresh coriander, which gives a unique citrus flavor to dishes and is often used as a topping.

Cotija: A dry, salty cheese often used as a topping.

Ensalada: Salad

Frijoles: Beans, usually pinto or black beans.

Hominy: Corn kernels that are soaked in lime to enable the removal of the germ and hull.

Jalapeño: A small green chile that is spicy hot

Masa: Fresh hominy ground into a dough.

Masa harina: Fresh masa that has been dried and then ground into a flour.

Nopales: Cactus

Pan: Bread

Pan dulce: Sweet bread

Poblano: A large dark green chile used as an ingredient in Mexican dishes.

Pollo: Chicken

Serrano: A small green chile that is slightly smaller than a jalapeno and about three times as hot.

Sopa: Soup. Also called caldo.

INDEX

INDEX

INDEX

INDEX